LEON

LEON

FAST & FREE

FREE-FROM RECIPES FOR
PEOPLE WHO REALLY LIKE FOOD

BY JANE BAXTER & JOHN VINCENT

conran
OCTOPUS

CONTENTS

LEON.
FAST & FREE

**THIS BOOK IS A BOOK FOR PEOPLE WHO WANT TO EAT WELL.
A FREE-FROM BOOK FOR PEOPLE WHO ACTUALLY LIKE FOOD.**

JOHN VINCENT

On one hand, this is the book that we should have written twelve years ago when we started LEON in 2004. It sums up why we began our adventure. We wanted to make it easy for everyone to eat well. On the other hand, the time for creating this book is now. Since we opened our first restaurant, our approach has gone from being radically alternative to almost mainstream.

From the start, we have believed in the power of food to delight, to invigorate, to bring people together. And we have believed too that the most healthy relationship with food is a positive and joyful one. But we also believe that modern industrialized food has made that relationship more opaque.

That is why at LEON, we aim to make it easier for people to eat well and steer clear of things that they are either temporarily, or permanently, avoiding. Every recipe in this book is gluten-, dairy-, and refined sugar-free. There are many other recipes which are nut-free, vegetarian, vegan, and even our version of paleo—Paleon.

You may be reading this because you have a serious medical condition and need to permanently avoid gluten, dairy, sugar, or something else entirely. You may be attempting to cut out or reduce your exposure to these things because you are sensitive to them. There is also an increasing number of people who for now, or for keeps, are aiming to "eat clean" to avoid the ingredients that can cause inflammation, or issues with the stomach and gut. Then there are the rest. People who don't care at all about this stuff and just want some tasty, exciting dishes to make life better. Well, you are welcome to this party, too.

We have debated how much time to spend on the science part. Not much, we concluded. The latest thinking on what we should cut back on, why, or when is available on your iphone or laptop (as are alternative views from people who think the opposite). There are professional, well trained, and well informed advisors who will help you get to the bottom of it, should you wish to. We've had lots of help along our free-from journey at LEON from nutritionists and food gurus. Our job, we concluded, is to help you with the how—how to cook without these things while still enjoying your food very much.

The world doesn't need too many more cookbooks in general. What it does need, we believe, is a free-from book that doesn't compromise on flavor, foodiness, or joy. A book that is naturally fast and naturally free. A book that sets you free to love cooking, and to enjoy eating and sharing your food with eagerness.

Within each section, there are broadly two types of dish: dishes that are naturally free-from (for example, recipes we have developed that would not in any case need wheat, dairy, or sugar); and dishes that typically rely on such ingredients (like cake) that we have reimagined to avoid or replace these ingredients.

We hope that you like the result. If we have done our job right, we will have created a very safe, but very fun playground for you. Somewhere you can play without concern, and do so with a skip in your step. This book is intended to set you free.

All our recipes are created to be fast as well as free. Some things may require patience, soaking overnight, or letting dough rest to prove, but there's no reason that eating freely should mean you can't have lots of stress-free free time. We begin with breakfast, and uncontroversially move on to appetizers, everyday easy lunches, and then speedy suppers. We have a dedicated section on sides and breads, and then go a bit more party-popper with appetizers and recipes for a crowd. Finally, to finish, it's all the tools you need to treat yourself. We wish you happy playing.

A WORD FROM JANE

As a professional cook who would quite happily dive face first into a vat of burrata or eat my body weight in grilled sourdough, I'm perhaps not the obvious choice to come up with a book of "free-from" recipes. To do that, the consensus seems to be that you have to be a glamorous ex model with thighs like a baby giraffe's and a penchant for spiralized zucchini, which, I hasten to add, I am not.

But this book is about the real world, not the airbrushed fantasy of glossy food magazines and advertising campaigns, and if there's one thing my 30-odd years in professional kitchens has taught me above all else, it's that the food you put on a plate has to taste fantastic if you're going win over an audience. That same philosophy is the guiding light for this, LEON's latest recipe collection. Many of the dishes you'll find in these

pages are influenced by my travels in southern Europe, southeastern Asia, and beyond, not least because there is an amazing number of food cultures out there in the wider world whose diet is naturally gluten- and dairy-free. Recipes such as Ethiopian flatbread using teff flour, fried tofu dumplings, and Asian shrimp pancakes are comforting, nourishing, and will make your tastebuds sing. But while we have focused on those far-flung corners for inspiration, we have also adapted all kinds of time-honored favorites from closer to home, to bring them into the "free-from" fold. So there's no need to mourn your favorite sticky toffee pudding or eggs Florentine now that you're embracing a new way of eating.

I'm so happy to be able to share them with you all. Here's to freedom.

NUTRITIONAL KEY

**Gluten-free, Dairy-free
& Refined Sugar-free**

**Low
Glycemic Load**

**Low
Saturated Fat**

Paleon

Nut-free

Vegetarian

Vegan

**Contains
Added Natural
Unrefined
Sugar***

**No Added
Sugar**

A WORD ON "PALEON"

We think that the premise of the paleo diet is a great one. Eating natural, unprocessed food inspired by our cavemen ancestors makes a lot of sense. At LEON, we've interpreted our own version of Paleo—Paleon. Many agree on the main principles of paleo but there are disagreements on the margins of how it should be applied. For example, vinegar is a big gray area. It's more processed than is normally okay for the paleo diet.

However, if it contains no added sugar and is consumed in relatively sparing amounts where it is crucial to the recipe, then we have let it go through. Similarly, paleo preaches a low-sugar diet, but if you want to make a Paleo dessert for special occasions and the like, palm sugar is a good natural, unrefined, low GL option. So again, we'll include it.

PALEON APROVED

FISH SAUCE

CURRY PASTE

SEA SALT

COCONUT AMINOS
a replacement for soy sauce

MUSTARD

STOCK

ARROWROOT POWDER

HERBS & SPICES

TAPIOCA FLOUR

UNSWEETENED COCOA

VANILLA

NATURAL SWEETENERS

MEAT

EGGS

FISH

FRUIT

SEEDS

VEGETABLES
sweet potatoes are okay

NUTS
not peanuts

QUINOA
another gray area that we approve

OILS & FATS
avocado, coconut, flaxseed, hazelnut, olive, ghee, sesame, walnut, macadamia, lard, tallow

WATER

HERBAL TEA

COFFEE

COCONUT WATER

FRESHLY JUICED FRUIT & VEG

CHIA SEEDS

NUTRITIONAL YEAST

PALEON NOT APROVED

PROCESSED FOODS

GRAINS:
wheat, corn, oats, rice, barley, millet, hops, spelt, rye, oats

LEGUMES:
all beans, chickpeas, lentils, peas, peanuts

SOY
edamame, tofu, etc.

POTATOES

SUGAR
gray area: raw okay by some

DAIRY

VEGETABLE OILS
peanut, canola, sunflower, corn, soybean, palm

ALCOHOL

YOUR
KITCHEN

CUPBOARD

WHY FREE-FROM?

From the inception of LEON we have labeled our dishes with icons that allow you to choose your food based on whether it is free from gluten or dairy, or on the extent to which it is likely to raise your blood sugar. Twelve years later, the interest in gluten, dairy, and sugar has grown considerably, both within nutritional science and in popular culture. Champion tennis players credit their success to eating free from gluten; TV presenters write books about how they feel having quit sugar; and most people have a friend who is ready to share their experience of eating "clean."

Beyond the anecdotal experiences and views of individuals is the scientific debate. We asked Meleni Aldridge, who specializes in reviewing the available science, to share her conclusions about what that science tells us. Not everyone will agree. And in fact for many people, even people with a suspicion that something is up, Meleni's conclusions may be quite controversial. Talk to us about it on Twitter, ask us questions, and take part in the debate.

Here are Meleni's conclusions. We hope they provide some new insights and some healthy food for thought.

MELENI ALDRIDGE BSc Nut Med, Dip cPNI

DAIRY, NOT THE STAPLE IT'S MADE OUT TO BE

Many people are increasingly turning away from dairy in search of alternatives that make them feel better, widen their diet, and help reduce our livestock burden on the planet, too. One of the most natural images in the world is that of a mother breastfeeding her baby and milk actually contains casomorphin, a feel-good component to ensure that babies keep coming back for more. This has a positive effect on the gut, calms the baby, and helps the mother-baby bonding process.

Milk is the perfect food for babies because an infant's gut produces lactase, the enzyme needed to break down lactose (milk sugar). Unfortunately lactase production drastically reduces after weaning, making lactose intolerance the most common, and well studied, carbohydrate intolerance in the world. Lactose intolerance is the root of much distress and ill health among many and, while certain people might benefit from the right kind of dairy products, others can just increase their susceptibility to dairy-driven health problems. Numerous scientific studies (which we won't get into here) have linked dairy consumption to a wealth of problems including irritable bowel syndrome, obesity, and autoimmune diseases. The body of literature is ever-growing and fascinating once you start reading it, but LEON are just here to help you enjoy a well rounded, deliciously dairy-free diet, whatever your motives.

REFINED SUGAR—GETTING OFF THE WHITE ROLLERCOASTER

You'll struggle to find a person among us who hasn't experienced a "sugar high," or its flip side, the "sugar low." Don't beat yourself up. Craving sugar is completely natural. Deep inside our genetic blueprint we're hardwired to seek out high-calorie foods and consume as much of them as we can. In fact, our very survival depended on this. Because these foods weren't readily available, it didn't matter if we gorged on them a few times a year. Today it's a different matter. With our encoded desire for sweet, sugary foods, coupled with their availability on every street corner, you need a pretty strong will to turn in the opposite direction. Here are some sugar facts to help you make better choices.

Energy and water are the only essential requisites for life – and staying alive is a high-energy business with every body system, organ, and cell demanding to be kept replete so it can function optimally. Sugar, like all carbohydrates, converts to glucose, which is one of the key fuels our body uses. Our body will turn to glucose if fuel from healthy fats and protein isn't available. In the energy hierarchy, when it comes to allocating glucose, your brain is top dog, so each time you indulge in too many sugary, simple-carb treats, you'll get a huge sugar rush that comes crashing down later. The desire to do it all over again then comes from your brain, which is starving because of a lack of energy-dense foods that fuel you for longer. Keeping this pattern going on a daily basis, year in and year out, puts us at much greater risk of type 2 diabetes, because our cells get more and more resistant to the insulin that the pancreas keeps pumping out in an effort to regulate blood sugar and mitigate the sugar rush and sugar crash. Enter the white rollercoaster of blood sugar imbalance.

Remember though that carbs, specifically complex carbs (slow-burning sugars), are critical for the body, and not just for energy but also to construct cell membranes, for our connective tissues, and for the metabolism of red blood cells. However, simple refined sugars (like sucrose and glucose) are fast fuels that are burned in minutes not hours. By not taking in sufficient protein, healthy fats, and complex carbs, we simply keep our brain in permanent request and craving mode.

Every recipe in this entire book is free from refined white table sugar. Instead, we've showcased a range of naturally occurring sugars like coconut sugar, maple syrup, rice malt, and raw honey, which come packed with good things from Nature's larder, including vitamins, minerals, antioxidants, trace elements, and enzymes. We've then used combinations with protein and healthy fats to further slow their release into the body, to help you to feel fuller, and save you from the turmoil of the white rollercoaster.

GLUTEN

All of a sudden the word gluten appears to be everywhere. The "free-from" aisle in the supermarket is dominated by gluten-free products and every third person you meet seems to want to avoid it.

SO WHAT IS GLUTEN?

Gluten is a family of proteins found in grains including wheat, rye, and barley. If you ever made play dough as a child you'll remember the sticky, glutinous, pliable, heavy mound that was formed as soon as you added water to a bowl full of flour. That pliable solidity is due to the gluten in the wheat flour, and this glutinous glue helps the foods made with these grains to hold their shape. But it can also wreak havoc in your gut—even if you don't feel a reaction.

FRIEND OR FOE?

Nature made our gut to behave best as a mostly sealed tube, with its own food factory (digestive processes), defense system (gut immune system), and friends and partners (gut bacteria). The gut is a fully functioning microcosm with the purpose of generating energy and maintaining life. In return for a happy home and the right foods and social conditions, our gut bacteria and other microbes do their best to work tirelessly for us, digesting, and creating compounds and cofactors with the aim of protecting us throughout our lives. The whole shebang is policed and kept in balance by the gut's immune system. Problems start occurring when the happy balance is disturbed. Gluten can interfere with the zonulin, a peptide that controls regulators (known as the

"tight junctions") between the internal gut and the body beyond. Zonulin is basically a gatekeeper, opening and closing the doors of the tight junctions to manage tiny molecules, both beneficial and harmful, within our gut and our bodies. When gluten interferes with the zonulin, the tube becomes "leaky" with the tight junctions thrown wide open.

None of this escapes detection by your body's immune system. It gets busy mobilizing a response, the strength and ferocity of which varies from individual to individual. Your immune system marks the gluten (as well as everything else floating out of your wide open tight junctions) as dangerous and creates a fire of inflammation to get rid of them. In some people the body's defense reaction to the leaked gut contents is swift and powerful, but in others it can take longer before causing symptoms.

FREE AT LAST

The solution to bring order and balance to this chaos is simple. Allow the natural regulation of our tight junctions to be restored by removing the trigger in our diets that causes the disruption. Current estimates suggest that while only 1 percent of Western populations are formally diagnosed with celiac disease, as many as 1 in 30 have a recognized sensitivity to gluten.

We're not saying gluten is the enemy and we're not telling you to avoid it entirely. Instead, we're offering you the option in this book to have completely gluten-free recipes, because we think they taste great that way.

1

GOOD MORNINGS

QUINOA FLORENTINE

Saturday morning magic. Go for a run first, and you will love yourself very much,
and maybe a few other people, too.

PREP TIME: 20 MINS · COOK TIME: 20 MINS

olive oil, for frying

¼ lb **spinach**

2 tablespoons **olive oil**

5½ oz **asparagus**, trimmed

4 **eggs**

FOR THE QUINOA FRITTERS:

1½ cups **quinoa**, cooked

1 **carrot**, grated

2 tablespoons **sesame seeds**

4 **scallions**, finely chopped

2 tablespoons chopped
   fresh parsley

2 **eggs**

1 teaspoon **tamari**

salt and **freshly ground black
   pepper**

FOR THE HOLLANDAISE:

3 **egg yolks** (room temperature)

1 tablespoon **water**

½ teaspoon **Dijon mustard**

½ teaspoon **whole grain mustard**

⅔ cup **olive oil** (not extra virgin)

1 tablespoon chopped
   fresh tarragon

1 tablespoon snipped **fresh chives**

lemon juice, to taste

1. Heat the oven to 250°F.

2. Mix the quinoa cake ingredients together to form a thick batter. Season well and set aside.

3. Place a heatproof bowl over gently simmering water and whisk the egg yolks with the water and mustards to combine. Gently warm the oil in a separate pan so it is roughly the same temperature as the eggs—it should be lukewarm if you put your finger into the pan. Slowly drizzle the oil into the eggs, whisking after each addition until you have a thick emulsion. Add the herbs, lemon juice to taste, and season well. Remove the pan from the heat, and the bowl from the simmering water, and set aside. Do not drain the water from the pan, as this can be used to blanch the asparagus and poach the eggs.

4. Heat the oil in a nonstick skillet and drop large spoonfuls of the quinoa mixture into the pan. You can make lots of small fritters or 4 large ones. Flatten with the back of a spoon and cook for 3 minutes on each side until browned and crisp. Place on a baking pan and keep warm in the oven.

5. Heat 1 tablespoon of olive oil in a large pan and add the spinach. Season well and stir vigorously until the spinach has wilted. Drain.

6. Blanch the asparagus in plenty of boiling water for 2 minutes. Drain and toss in a little olive oil. Season well and keep warm in the oven.

7. Poach the eggs in simmering water for about 3 minutes. Remove from the pan and drain well.

8. To serve, top the quinoa fritters with spinach and asparagus. Place a poached egg on top and serve drizzled with the hollandaise.

Purple sprouting broccoli would also go well with this dish. If you want to make it paleo, swap the tamari for coconut aminos and the rice bran oil for olive oil.

COCONUT MANGO PANCAKES

(NF)

(V)

These taste like an all-inclusive tropical honeymoon. In a nice clean way. These thin, crisp pancakes are also delightful with pineapple and banana.

PREP TIME: 10 MINS · COOK TIME: 10 MINS

½ cup **desiccated coconut**

⅓ cup **rice flour**

½ cup **cornstarch**

1 **egg**

1 tablespoon **coconut milk**

½ cup **water**

a pinch of **salt**

a drop of **vanilla extract**

¼ cup **coconut sugar**

1 tablespoon **grapeseed oil**

1 **mango**

1. Cover the desiccated coconut with boiling water and set aside.

2. Sift the flour and cornstarch into a large bowl. Beat together the egg, coconut milk, and water. Add the wet mixture slowly to the flour until you have a thin batter. Stir in the salt and vanilla.

3. Drain the desiccated coconut and squeeze out any excess moisture. Heat a nonstick skillet and dry-toast the coconut over medium heat with the sugar until it has caramelized slightly. Remove from the pan and wipe clean.

4. Heat the oil in the pan and pour a small ladleful of the batter into the center, tilting the pan to make a thin pancake. Cook for a minute on either side, then remove from the pan and repeat until you have used up all the batter and have a pile of pancakes.

5. Peel the mango and cut it into chunks or thin slices.

6. Serve each pancake with a little toasted coconut and mango.

Don't be sad when your first pancake doesn't turn out well. It was always thus.

BUCKWHEAT CRÊPES

When first getting to grips with eating gluten free, whether or not you can eat buckwheat always seems like a trick question. It is in fact, a trick-free, gluten-free grass, and delightful served either savory or sweet. We've served them here as a crêpe suzette, by segmenting a few blood oranges, sprinkling them with coconut sugar, and finishing them off in the pan with a splash of Cointreau. However, we'd also suggest serving them with cashew béchamel (see page 92) and cooked cabbage, or with the mushroom sauce from the lasagne (see page 174).

PREP TIME: 10 MINS · COOK TIME: 15 MINS

1 cup **buckwheat flour**

a pinch of **salt**

1 **egg**

1¼ cups **almond milk**

2 teaspoons **pumpkin seed oil**

olive oil, for frying

blood oranges, to serve (see introduction above)

1. Sift the flour and salt into a bowl. Whisk the egg and add it to the almond milk, along with the pumpkin seed oil.

2. Slowly pour the wet ingredients into the dry, beating until you have a smooth batter.

3. Heat a tablespoon of oil in a nonstick skillet. Pour a small ladleful of the batter into the pan, tilting it so you have a thin layer covering the pan surface. Cook for a minute, then flip the crêpe over and cook for another minute on the other side.

4. Repeat with the rest of the batter and serve with the blood oranges.

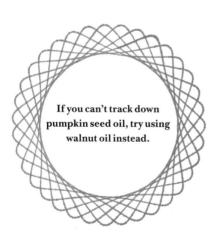

If you can't track down pumpkin seed oil, try using walnut oil instead.

POHA

Poha is flattened, beaten, or flaked rice, and you can buy it in Asian and Indian supermarkets, or online. If you can't find it, basmati rice will still be delicious. A traditional home-cooked Indian breakfast, its full flavor and fluffy lightness will fill you up for the day.

PREP TIME: 10 MINS · SOAK TIME: 15 MINS · COOK TIME: 15 MINS

⅔ cup **poha**

½ teaspoon **salt**

juice of ½ **lime**

½ teaspoon **ground turmeric**

½ teaspoon **chili powder**

1 tablespoon **rice bran oil**

2 teaspoons **mustard seeds**

½ teaspoon **cumin seeds**

1 **red onion**, chopped

2 **green chiles**, chopped

10 **curry leaves**

1 **beefsteak tomato**, skinned, seeded, and chopped

1 **zucchini**, chopped

2 tablespoons **sliced almonds**

salt and **freshly ground black pepper**

chopped **fresh cilantro**, to serve

1. Rinse the poha in lots of cold water. Drain and cover with more water. Set aside for about 15 minutes, then drain again and break up any lumps. Add the salt, lime, turmeric, and chili powder, and mix well.

2. Heat the oil in a large pan. Add the mustard and cumin seeds, and, when they start to pop, tip in the onion, green chiles, and curry leaves. Stir-fry until the onions start to brown.

3. Add the tomato and zucchini. Cook for another 5 minutes, then add the poha and almonds. Stir-fry over medium heat for another 5 minutes.

4. Check the seasoning and serve topped with chopped cilantro.

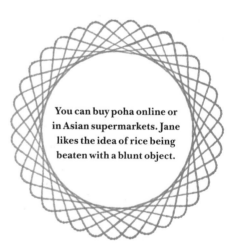

You can buy poha online or in Asian supermarkets. Jane likes the idea of rice being beaten with a blunt object.

BANAN-ALMOND PANCAKES

Don't let Shrove Tuesday "crêpe up" on you—practice by eating pancakes way more often. Jane likes making these for her son. Jane likes her son. Even if he did give her a package of Viennese cookies for Mother's Day, only for her to find the empty package of cookies in his room later.

PREP TIME: 10 MINS
COOK TIME: 10 MINS

2 ripe **bananas**
1 **egg**
½ cup **almond milk**
1 tablespoon **raw honey**, plus extra
   to serve
1 teaspoon **vanilla extract**
½ cup **almond flour**
⅔ cup **rice flour**
a pinch of **ground cinnamon**
1 teaspoon **baking powder**
a pinch of **baking soda**
a pinch of **salt**
canola oil, for frying

1. Blend the bananas with the egg, milk, honey, and vanilla in a food processor, or mash well with a fork.

2. Sift together the dry ingredients in a large bowl. Slowly add the wet ingredients and stir until you have a thick batter.

3. Heat a tablespoon of oil in a large nonstick skillet. Drop tablespoons of the batter into the skillet and cook for 2 minutes on each side, until lightly browned.

4. Repeat until all the batter is used and serve drizzled with honey.

Serve with fresh berries, or any fruit that takes your fancy, and raw organic honey.

WHITE CRABMEAT OMELET

This tastes of a bright and peaceful morning in Koh Samui—or one of those smaller islands next door. It's a super-light omelet with a filling Pad Thai seasoning.

PREP TIME: 10 MINS · COOK TIME: 10 MINS

juice of 1 **lime**

2 tablespoons **fish sauce**, plus 2 teaspoons

1 tablespoon **coconut sugar**

1 teaspoon **tamarind paste**

1 teaspoon **chili sauce**

3 tablespoons **rice bran oil**, divided

1 clove of **garlic**, crushed

6 **eggs**

a large pinch of **ground white pepper**

7 oz **white crabmeat**

½ cup **beansprouts**

a handful of **pea shoots** or **watercress**

½ **daikon radish**, julienned

⅓ cup **toasted peanuts**, chopped coarsely

a small bunch of **chives**, snipped into pieces ¾ to 1¼ inches long

2 tablespoons fresh **cilantro leaves**

1. Mix together the lime juice, 2 tablespoons of fish sauce, the coconut sugar, tamarind paste, and chili sauce to make your dressing. Set aside.

2. Heat 1 tablespoon of rice bran oil in a large nonstick skillet or wok. Add the garlic to the pan and quickly stir-fry, then add the dressing. Bring to a simmer and cook for a few minutes until the mixture has reduced and become syrupy. Take it off the heat and let cool.

3. Clean the pan, then heat the remaining oil. Whisk the eggs with the 2 teaspoons of fish sauce and the pepper. Pour half the egg mixture into the pan, tilting the pan to make a thin layer. Cook for 1 minute, then transfer to a plate—do not turn the omelet over. Repeat with the remaining egg mixture.

4. To serve, divide the crab between the omelets and scatter with the beansprouts, pea shoots (or watercress), daikon radish, peanuts, and herbs. Drizzle with the syrupy dressing, fold the omelets over, and slice each one in half to serve.

> **White crab meat comes from the claws and legs of the crab. Delicate and sweet in flavor, crab meat is very low in fat and high in protein.**

SWEET POTATO QUESADILLAS WITH EGGS & AVOCADO

Let's start by clarifying that there's no queso in these dillas—but we challenge you to describe these tortilla packages any other way. We've used a combination of plain and blue corn tortillas here—we think they're beautiful. Your enjoyment of these should not be limited to breakfast, but it's a good place to start.

PREP TIME: 15 MINS · COOK TIME: 25 MINS

2 small **sweet potatoes** (or 1 large)

a pinch of **smoked paprika**

1 **shallot**, chopped

1 **green chile**, chopped

2 tablespoons chopped
  fresh cilantro, plus extra
  to serve

1 **cob of corn**, cooked and
  kernels sliced off and reserved

juice of 1 **lime**, divided

2 **avocados**, coarsely chopped

½ clove of **garlic**, crushed

3 tablespoons **olive oil**, divided

8 small **corn tortillas**
  (see page 248)

4 **eggs**

salt and **cayenne pepper**

1. Heat the oven to 250°F.

2. Peel the sweet potatoes and slice thinly, using a mandoline slicer if you have one. Steam for about 15 minutes, or until tender. Let cool, then fold through the paprika, shallot, chile, cilantro, cooked kernels of corn, and half the lime juice. Season well.

3. Mix the avocado with the rest of the lime juice, the crushed garlic, and 1 tablespoon of the olive oil. Season well.

4. Lay 4 corn tortillas on a clean surface. Spread the sweet potato mixture evenly over the tortillas and top each with another tortilla.

5. Heat 1 tablespoon of oil in a nonstick skillet and fry the tortillas one at a time for a minute on each side, being careful not to lose any filling when you flip them over. Transfer each tortilla to a baking pan in the preheated oven to keep warm. Alternatively, you can grill them for a minute on each side.

6. Fry the eggs in the leftover oil to your liking. To plate up, top each quesadilla with a fried egg and some of the avocado. Scatter with extra cilantro to serve.

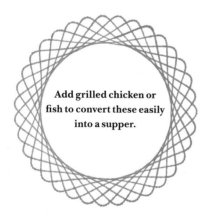

Add grilled chicken or fish to convert these easily into a supper.

CAULI KEDGEREE

Now for a modern version of a very British breakfast. The cauliflower couscous packs more plants into your morning. Caul me, maybe?

PREP TIME: 15 MINS · COOK TIME: 25 MINS

1 **cauliflower**

1 lb 2 oz **smoked haddock fillet**

2 tablespoons **canola oil**

1 **onion**, finely chopped

2 **leeks**, sliced

a pinch of **saffron**

a pinch of **ground cardamom**

1 clove of **garlic**, crushed

1 × ¾-inch piece of **ginger**, grated

1 **red chile**, chopped

1 teaspoon **curry powder**

2 teaspoons **nigella seeds**

¾ cup **peas**, cooked

2 tablespoons chopped **fresh parsley**, plus extra to serve

4 **eggs**, boiled to your liking

2 tablespoons **sliced almonds**, toasted

salt and **freshly ground black pepper**

1. Blitz the cauliflower florets in a food processor or grate on a fine grater until they resemble couscous.

2. Grill the fish for a few minutes until just cooked, then flake it into large pieces using 2 forks, or your fingers.

3. Heat the oil in a large pan and cook the onion for 5 minutes over low heat. Add the leeks, saffron, and cardamom and cook for another 5 minutes before adding the garlic, ginger, and chile. Cook for 2 minutes, then add the cauliflower, curry powder, and nigella seeds.

4. Stir well and cook for another 5 minutes, making sure the cauliflower doesn't stick. Fold in the peas, fish, and chopped parsley and heat through.

5. Check the seasoning and serve garnished with the boiled eggs, toasted almonds, and extra chopped parsley.

QUINOA KITCHARI

Kitchari was the inspiration for kedgeree (which sounds like a hungover Englishman trying to pronounce it). This will soak up any sins the morning after, and leave you feeling virtually virtuous.

**PREP TIME: 10 MINS · SOAK TIME: OVERNIGHT
COOK TIME: 25 MINS**

½ cup **split mung beans**

1 cup **quinoa**

1 tablespoon **rice bran oil**

2 teaspoons **black mustard seeds**

2 teaspoons **crushed fennel seeds**

3 **cardamom pods**

1 × ¾-inch **stick of cinnamon**

½ teaspoon each **ground cumin** and **coriander**

a pinch of **ground turmeric**

1 × ¾-inch piece of **ginger**, grated

1 quart **water** or **vegetable stock**

¾ cup **peas**

⅔ cup **edamame beans**

⅔ cup **fava beans**

1¾ cups diced **zucchini**

¼ lb **spinach**, shredded

1 tablespoon chopped **cilantro**

salt and **freshly ground black pepper**

1. Soak the split mung beans overnight in plenty of cold water. Rinse the quinoa thoroughly. Drain both the mung beans and quinoa very well.

2. Heat the oil in a large saucepan and cook the spices for a minute, stirring well before adding the quinoa and mung beans. Cook for a minute, stirring well, and season. Add the water or stock. Bring up to a simmer and cook (covered) over very low heat for 15 minutes, until the quinoa is cooked through and the dal is soft.

3. Put the vegetables into a steamer, season, and let stand for 5 minutes over low heat to steam. Turn the heat off and fold the vegetables through the dal and quinoa. Cover and let stand for 10 minutes.

4. Serve garnished with fresh cilantro.

ALMOND MILK PORRIDGE
WITH BANANA & CINNAMON

This porridge is just right. At Leon, we sell about 172,000 pounds of porridge a year. That's the equivalent of 40 elephants, 6 double-decker buses, or a Concorde. And just as fast.

PREP TIME: 5 MINS · COOK TIME: 10 MINS

1 cup **gluten-free rolled oats**

2 cups **unsweetened almond milk**

1 tablespoon **date and vanilla purée** (see below)

2 to 3 **bananas**

ground cinnamon, to garnish

1. Cook the oats with the almond milk in a small nonstick saucepan over low heat, stirring very regularly for around 10 minutes, or until it has reached your desired consistency. We think it should be creamy, but not mushy.

2. Serve your porridge with a generous dollop of the date and vanilla purée, some slices of banana, and a light dusting of cinnamon.

DATE & VANILLA PURÉE

PREP TIME: 5 MINS · MAKES A 7-OUNCE JAR

3½ oz **medjool dates** (stones removed)

½ cup **water**

seeds from 1 **vanilla bean**

1. Put all the ingredients into a blender and blitz until completely smooth.

2. This will make more than you need (approximately 10 portions), but it will keep fresh in your fridge for up to 7 days. It is also great spread on your nutty seedy loaf (see page 42).

We sometimes replace ½ cup of the milk with water, to make it less rich. You can also scatter the porridge with some toasted seeds or chopped nuts if you want to add some crunch.

TRUFFLE-CODDLED EGGS

A luxurious Sunday morning treat. Totally worth the truffle.
Thank you to our friend Brad for the inspiration.

PREP TIME: 20 MINS · COOK TIME: 35 MINS

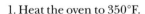

7 oz **Jerusalem artichokes**

2 tablespoons **olive oil**, divided

1¼ cups sliced **cremini mushrooms**

½ clove of **garlic**, crushed

leaves from 1 sprig of **fresh thyme**

1¾ oz **kale**, cooked

4 **eggs**

1 tablespoon snipped **fresh chives**

a drizzle of **truffle oil**

salt and **freshly ground black pepper**

1. Heat the oven to 350°F.

2. Peel the Jerusalem artichokes and slice them thinly. Heat 1 tablespoon of oil in a small pan and add the artichokes. Cook for a few minutes over high heat. Season well and cover. Lower the heat and let cook gently for about 10 minutes, or until they are soft. Blitz until smooth with a hand-held stick blender or in a food processor and set aside.

3. Heat the rest of the oil in a skillet. Cook the mushrooms with the garlic and thyme for 5 minutes until softened. Season well.

4. Chop the kale and season well.

5. Take 4 ramekins and divide the kale among them. Top with the mushrooms and finish with the artichoke purée. Make an indentation in the purée and crack an egg into each ramekin. Season with salt and pepper.

6. Place the ramekins in a baking dish and pour in boiling water so that it comes three-quarters up the side of the ramekins. This makes a water bath, and ensures that everything cooks evenly and doesn't become rubbery. Transfer (carefully) to the oven and bake for about 15 to 20 minutes, depending on how you like your eggs cooked.

7. Remove from the oven, scatter with the chives, and drizzle with the truffle oil before serving.

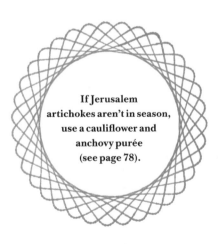

If Jerusalem
artichokes aren't in season,
use a cauliflower and
anchovy purée
(see page 78).

SMASHED FAVA BEANS, KALE & HAM

You can make this recipe with shredded ham, but by cooking the ham hock you get a better result, along with some extra stock to make soup. I think, therefore I ham.

PREP TIME: 15 MINS · SOAK TIME: 1 HOUR · COOK TIME: 1 HOUR

1 **ham hock**

vegetables for stock (**onion**, **celery**, **leek**, **carrot** trimmings)

1 **onion**, chopped

2 tablespoons **olive oil**

2 cups **fava beans** (frozen are fine)

1 clove of **garlic**, thinly sliced

a pinch of **chile flakes**

¼ lb **kale**, cooked and chopped

4 **eggs**

white wine vinegar

1 tablespoon shredded **fresh mint**

salt and **freshly ground black pepper**

1 tablespoon chopped **fresh parsley**

a drizzle of **olive oil**, to serve

1. Soak the ham hock in cold water for an hour. Drain and place in a pressure cooker along with some stock vegetables, such trimmings of onions, celery, leeks, and carrots (or just use vegetable stock).

2. Bring up to steam and cook over medium heat for 40 minutes. This step can be done in a normal pan but will take more than 3 hours.

3. Let the ham hock cool down in the stock. Drain, reserving the cooking liquor. Shred about 5½ ounces of the ham hock meat and set aside. The rest of the ham will keep in the refrigerator for up to 4 days.

4. Cook the chopped onion in a little oil for 10 minutes until soft. Add the fava beans and stir well to combine. Add 1¾ cups of the ham stock and let simmer for 5 minutes or until the beans are soft. Place half the mixture in a food processor and blitz to chop coarsely. Return the mixture to the pan and fold together with the rest of the beans. Season with black pepper.

5. Heat the rest of the oil in a small pan. Add the garlic and chile flakes and cook for 2 minutes until fragrant but without coloring. Add the chopped kale and braise together for 2 minutes. Fold in the reserved 5½ ounces of shredded ham hock.

6. Poach the eggs in plenty of simmering water containing a good glug of vinegar for about 4 minutes. Let drain on a plate lined with paper towels.

7. Fold the mint through the fava beans, then on each plate place a little of the smashed beans and braised kale. Top with a poached egg, scatter with parsley, and drizzle with olive oil to serve.

HIP HOPPERS
WITH FOUR TOPPERS

🍴④

This Sri Lankan fermented rice batter makes enough for 8 egg hoppers (2 each) plus a few extra pancakes. You have to start this recipe the day before, so the batter has time to develop or ferment. The hoppers are traditionally cooked in small, high-sided pans, but a deep small nonstick pan will do. As with pancakes, the first few may not work, but do persevere. We find that they cook better on a gas stove where the heat goes up the sides of the pan. Any (or all) of the accompaniments overleaf are great with the hoppers. Hop to it.

PREP TIME: 15 MINS · STAND TIME: OVERNIGHT · COOK TIME: 2 TO 3 MINS

3 tablespoons **coconut water**

½ teaspoon **active dry yeast**

½ teaspoon **sugar**

⅔ cup **coconut milk**

⅔ cup **brown rice flour**

3 tablespoons **soda water**, plus extra

a large pinch of **salt**

canola oil

8 **eggs**

1. Heat the coconut water until tepid, but not hot (you don't want to kill the yeast). Don't be afraid to stick your finger into the pan. Whisk in the yeast and sugar and let stand off the heat for 15 minutes. Stir in the coconut milk. Put the rice flour into a large bowl and pour in the coconut mixture. Beat until you have a smooth batter. Cover with plastic wrap and let stand overnight.

2. In the morning, add the soda water and beat well. Season with the salt. Let stand for an hour before using—it should be thinner than a traditional pancake batter. If it has thickened on standing, or if your coconut milk was very thick, add some extra soda water until it is the consistency of light cream.

3. Heat your pan and pour some oil into a bowl. Dip a clean cloth into the oil and use it to grease the pan. Slowly pour a small ladleful of the batter into the pan, tilting it so that the batter coats up the inside edge of the pan and is distributed in a thin layer. Quickly crack an egg into the bottom of the pan on top of the pancake and cover. Let cook for about 2 minutes or until the egg is just cooked and the pancake is starting to brown around the edges. Run a metal spatula around the inside edge of the pan and ease the hopper onto a plate.

4. Repeat with the remaining batter and eggs. Any extra can be saved or cooked plain without eggs.

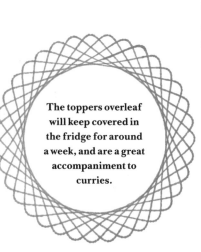

The toppers overleaf will keep covered in the fridge for around a week, and are a great accompaniment to curries.

COCONUT GRAVY

1 **onion**, sliced
2 cloves of **garlic**, crushed
½ teaspoon **ground turmeric**
½ teaspoon **ground fenugreek seeds**
1 × ¾-inch stick of **cinnamon**
3 **green chiles**, coarsely chopped
10 **curry leaves**
1¾ cups **coconut milk**
juice of ½ **lime**
salt

PREP TIME: 5 MINS · COOK TIME: 15 MINS
ENOUGH FOR 8 HOPPERS

1. Place all the ingredients, apart from the lime juice and salt, in a pan. Put over medium heat and bring up to a simmer. Cook gently for about 15 minutes, or until the onions have softened and the gravy has thickened.

2. Season well and add lime juice to taste.

GREEN SAMBAL

3 tablespoons **desiccated coconut**
2 tablespoons chopped **fresh parsley**
a handful of **kale leaves**, finely shredded
2 large **shallots**, finely chopped
3 **green chiles**, finely chopped
1 tablespoon **lime juice**
salt

PREP TIME: 5 MINS · STAND TIME: 15 MINS
ENOUGH FOR 8 HOPPERS

1. Cover the coconut with boiling water and let stand for about 15 minutes. Place in a sieve and lightly press to remove excess water.

2. Mix with the other ingredients in a bowl and season well.

SEENI SAMBAL

2 tablespoons **rice bran oil**
1 × ¾-inch stick of **cinnamon**
2 **cloves**
3 **cardamom pods**, crushed
3 **red onions**, finely chopped
2 sprigs of **fresh curry leaves**
1 tablespoon **red chile flakes**
2 teaspoons **coconut sugar**
1 teaspoon **tamarind paste**
salt and **freshly ground black pepper**

PREP TIME: 5 MINS · COOK TIME: 20 MINS
ENOUGH FOR 8 HOPPERS

1. Heat the oil in a large pan. Add the cinnamon, cloves, and cardamom pods. Cook for a minute, stirring. Add the onions, curry leaves, and red chile flakes and cook for 10 minutes over low heat without browning them.

2. Stir in the sugar and tamarind paste and mix well. Cook slowly for another 10 minutes, adding a little water if the onions start to stick. Season well.

LUNU MIRIS

1 large **red onion**, finely chopped
2 tablespoons **red chile flakes**
2 **red chiles**, finely chopped
1 tablespoon **lime juice**
salt

PREP TIME: 5 MINS · ENOUGH FOR 8 HOPPERS

1. Mix the chopped onion with the dried and fresh chiles. Pound them together in a mortar and pestle (or give them a quick pulse in a food processor).

2. Place in a bowl and mix with the lime juice and salt.

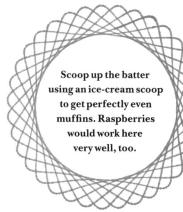

Scoop up the batter using an ice-cream scoop to get perfectly even muffins. Raspberries would work here very well, too.

BLUEBERRY MUFFINS

A little bit of berried treasure to discover at breakfast. They're so easy to make, there's really muffin to it. This is a recipe from our friends Meleni and Rob from the Alliance of Natural Health.

PREP TIME: 10 MINS · COOK TIME: 20 MINS

½ cup **coconut oil**, melted, plus extra for greasing

4 **eggs**, beaten

1 teaspoon **vanilla extract**

⅓ cup **rice malt syrup**

⅓ cup **almond milk**

2 cups **almond flour**

2 teaspoons **baking powder**

½ teaspoon **salt**

⅔ cup **blueberries** (frozen are fine if fresh aren't in season)

1. Heat the oven to 350°F.

2. Grease a muffin pan and set it aside, or line the pan with paper muffin cups, if you prefer. Sift together all the dry ingredients.

3. Beat the wet ingredients together and stir into the dry ingredients.

4. Fold through the blueberries. Add a scoop of batter to each hole of the muffin pan and bake for about 15 to 20 minutes, or until a skewer inserted in the center of a muffin comes out clean. Leave to cool before serving.

NUTTY SEEDY LOAF

Be the breadwinner with this loaf. It makes great toast, and keeps for about a week. Flaxseeds, chia seeds, and psyllium husks help the dough stretch and mimic the properties of gluten. Jane came up with this recipe and when she shared it, John was excited to see that it was very similar to a recipe that his friends Louka and Wendy had made for him on their trip to Lamu. So this is dedicated to Wendy and Louka, two of the wisest people John knows.

PREP TIME: 10 MINS · COOK TIME: 1 HOUR 10 MINS

½ cup **pumpkin seeds**

½ cup **sunflower seeds**

⅓ cup **sesame seeds**

1 cup **almond flour**

1 cup **buckwheat flour**

1 cup **gluten-free oats**

¼ cup **flaxseeds**

2 tablespoons **ground psyllium husks**

2 tablespoons **ground chia seeds**

3 tablespoons **olive oil**

2 tablespoons **rice malt syrup**

2 cups **water**

1 teaspoon **salt**

1. Heat the oven to 325°F.

2. Place the pumpkin, sunflower, and sesame seeds on a baking pan in the oven and toast for 10 minutes, until lightly browned. Place in a bowl. When cool, mix them with the two flours, oats, flaxseeds, psyllium, and chia seeds.

3. Mix the wet ingredients with the salt and beat to blend together. Pour into the dry ingredients and beat with a spoon to make sure everything is mixed together thoroughly.

4. Line a 9 x 5 inch loaf pan with nonstick parchment paper. Pour the mixture into the pan and flatten down with the back of a spoon. Cover and let rest overnight in the fridge.

5. Once rested, heat your oven to 400°F. Take the pan out of the fridge and let the loaf return to room temperature. Bake in the oven for an hour, then transfer to a cooling rack and let cool completely before turning out of the pan. The loaf will keep well in a sealed container and tastes fabulous toasted and spread with soy spread.

2

FOR STARTERS

PUFFED RICE
WITH PORK & SHRIMP DIP

Posh rice cakes with a rich satay-style sauce. Make a few extra bunches of puffed rice pieces and top them with almond butter and bananas for breakfast. The trick to making them hold their shape is to really squash the rice down. Putting a sheet of nonstick parchment paper or plastic wrap on top stops your hands from getting sticky and let's you really go for it until it's super compact.

PREP TIME: 15 MINS · COOK TIME: 1 HOUR, 10 MINS

1 cup **jasmine rice**

2 cups **water**

salt

1 tablespoon **coconut oil**

5½ oz **ground pork**

5½ oz **raw shrimp meat**, chopped

2 **shallots**, finely chopped

1 tablespoon **chopped cilantro stalks**

1 clove of **garlic**, crushed

2 teaspoons **ground white pepper**

2 tablespoons **fish sauce**

2 teaspoons **tamarind paste**

1 tablespoon **palm sugar**

1 cup **coconut milk**

⅓ cup **roasted peanuts**, ground

1 teaspoon **fish paste** (**balachan**)

rice bran oil, for frying

1. Put the rice and water into a pan together along with a pinch of salt. Bring to a boil, then turn the heat down and simmer for about 20 minutes, until all the water has been absorbed.

2. Tip the rice onto a baking pan lined with nonstick parchment paper. Place another sheet of parchment paper on top and press down on it firmly until you have a thin layer of rice. Remove the top sheet and cut the rice into small square cakes with a knife. Let cool. Dry the rice cakes in an oven preheated to 180°F for about 30 minutes. Flip the cakes over and return them to the oven until completely dry. Store in a sealed container until needed.

3. Heat the coconut oil in a large skillet. Fry the pork until lightly browned. Remove with a slotted spoon. Fry the shrimp meat for a few minutes and add to the pork. Cook the shallots with the cilantro, garlic, and pepper for a few minutes. Blitz the pork and shrimp in a food processor, then return to the pan and stir well over low heat for 5 minutes. Add the fish sauce, tamarind, sugar, and coconut milk. Bring the mixture up to a simmer and cook gently for 5 minutes. Stir in the peanuts and fish paste and season well.

4. Heat some oil (about ¾ inch deep) in a pan. Fry the rice cakes in batches until puffed and golden brown. Serve with the pork and shrimp dip.

OKA(Y)

4

Oka is a Samoan variation of poke that you can buy as a street snack served in a plastic cup. Bill and Ross gave Jane this recipe from their restaurant, Bistro Tatau, where Jane worked while she was pregnant.

PREP TIME: 15 MINS · CURE TIME: 20 MINS

1 lb 2 oz **gurnard** or **bream fillets,** boned and skinned, cut into ¾-inch chunks

juice of 4 **limes**

2 large **tomatoes,** skinned, seeded, and cut into fine dice

4 **scallions,** finely chopped

1 small **red onion,** finely chopped

1 **red chile,** chopped

½ **cucumber,** peeled, seeded, and finely chopped

1¼ cups **coconut cream**

2 tablespoons chopped **fresh cilantro**

salt and **freshly ground black pepper**

1. Place the fish in a glass bowl and cover with the lime juice. Sprinkle with salt and let stand for 20 minutes to "cook."

2. Drain the fish and mix with the diced and chopped vegetables in a large bowl. Fold in the coconut cream and season well.

3. Serve in a glass bowl or a plastic cup and top with the chopped cilantro.

HOKEY POKE

6

This Hawaiian dish is traditionally made with very fresh yellowfin tuna, but salmon is a good substitute.

PREP TIME: 15 MINS

1 lb 2 oz **salmon** (or **tuna**) **fillet**

2 teaspoons **sesame oil**

2 teaspoons finely grated **ginger**

2 teaspoons **tamari**

1 **red chile,** seeded and finely chopped

1 tablespoon **toasted sesame seeds**

½ **kohlrabi,** cut into fine strips (or julienne)

1 bunch of **scallions,** cut into strips

cilantro leaves, to garnish

2 teaspoons **black sesame seeds,** to garnish

1. Cut the fish into ¾-inch chunks.

2. Mix together the sesame oil, ginger, tamari, chile, and toasted sesame seeds. Add the fish chunks and toss gently in the marinade to coat.

3. Scatter the kohlrabi and scallions on a serving dish. Place the marinaded fish on top and scatter with the cilantro leaves and black sesame seeds to serve.

Any firm white-fleshed fish can be used in this dish. It also works well with the fruity addition of 10½ ounces ripe, sliced papaya at the bottom of the serving cups.

SHRIMP SUMMER ROLLS

These make a punchy and aromatic appetizer, or a tidy snack for a summer picnic.

PREP TIME: 35 MINS

1¾ oz **vermicelli rice noodles**

1 teaspoon **sesame oil**

8 **lettuce leaves**

basil and **mint leaves**, about 24
(3 for each roll)

8 **cilantro sprigs**

16 **cooked jumbo shrimp**

8 **ricepaper wrappers**

ALL CUT INTO FINE STRIPS

1 **carrot**

½ **red bell pepper**

¼ **cucumber**

6 **sugar snap peas**

¼ **daikon radish** or **kohlrabi**

1. Cover the noodles with boiling water for about 2 minutes or until they are al dente. Drain and refresh. Cut into smaller pieces and toss in sesame oil.

2. Lay out the lettuce leaves and top each one with the herbs, strips of vegetables, and a little of the noodles. Top each one with 2 shrimp.

3. Soak one ricepaper wrapper in warm water until soft and pliable. Place on a damp cloth and top with one of the filled lettuce leaves, then roll up as tightly as possible, folding in the sides to make a parcel. Repeat with the rest of the wrappers.

4. To serve, slice each roll in half diagonally and serve with nuoc cham dipping sauce (see below).

NUOC CHAM DIPPING SAUCE

PREP TIME: 15 MINS · COOK TIME: 5 MINS · COOL TIME: 5 MINS

1 tablespoon **rice vinegar**

1 tablespoon **palm sugar**

2 tablespoons **water**

2 **red chiles**, seeded and finely chopped

1 clove of **garlic**, crushed

2 tablespoons **fish sauce** (or **tamari** for vegetarians)

juice of 1 **lime**

cilantro leaves

1. In a saucepan bring the vinegar, palm sugar, and water to a boil. Let cool, then add the rest of the dipping sauce ingredients. This will keep in a sealed container in the refrigerator for up to 4 days.

These also work well if you make them completely vegetarian, or you could use duck, pork, or rare beef. If you want a lighter option, use shredded daikon radish or kohlrabi instead of the noodles.

FOUR-STYLE CURED SALMON

In search of a cure for salmon, we made these four. Fancy a fifth? Try serving it with the hollandaise on page 16 for an eggs royale worthy of the Queen. Below is how to cure the salmon, and opposite are our suggestions for how to enjoy it.

PREP TIME: 5 MINS · CURE TIME: 2 DAYS

1 lb 2 oz piece of **salmon**, skin on, bone removed

3 tablespoons **sea salt**

2 tablespoons **raw honey**

2 tablespoons chopped **fresh dill**

1 teaspoon **ground white pepper**

2 tablespoons **Sambuca** or other **aniseed liqueur** (optional)

1. Cut the salmon in half horizontally. Mix the salt with the honey, Sambuca, dill, and pepper and spread over the flesh of the salmon halves. Sandwich the pieces together and seal in plastic wrap. Place in a nonmetallic dish with a weight on top. This could be a can or anything that will apply a little pressure to the salmon.

2. Place in the fridge for about 36 hours, turning the fish over every 8 hours. Remove from the plastic wrap and wipe with paper towels. To serve, slice the salmon thinly.

1.

2.

3.

4.

1. CUCUMBER & DILL SALAD WITH MUSTARD SAUCE

PREP TIME: 10 MINS · SALT TIME: 30 MINS

1 **cucumber**, peeled and seeded

1 tablespoon **apple cider vinegar**, plus 2 teaspoons

1 teaspoon **coconut sugar**

2 tablespoons snipped **fresh chives**

1 tablespoon **Dijon mustard**

1 tablespoon **raw honey**

1 tablespoon finely chopped **fresh dill**

2 tablespoons **grapeseed oil**

cured salmon, thinly sliced (see opposite)

1 bunch of **watercress**

salt

1. Slice the cucumber into thin strips. Sprinkle with salt and let stand in a colander for about 30 minutes. Pat dry and toss with 2 teaspoons of the apple cider vinegar, the sugar, and chives.

2. Blend together the mustard, honey, dill, oil, and remaining 1 tablespoon of vinegar.

3. To serve, arrange the salmon to one side of each plate and drizzle with the dressing. Pile up the cucumber salad to the other side, with some of the watercress.

2. BELGIAN ENDIVE, CELERY ROOT & CAPERS

PREP TIME: 15 MINS · SOAK TIME: 20 MINS

2 heads of **red Belgian endive**

½ lb **celery root**, peeled and grated

1 tablespoon **olive oil**

1 teaspoon **fresh tarragon**, finely chopped

cured salmon, thinly sliced (see opposite)

2 tablespoons **capers**, soaked for about 20 minutes

1 small **red onion**, thinly sliced

1. Separate the leaves of the endive and arrange on a plate. Toss the celery root with the oil and tarragon, and scatter it onto the endive leaves.

2. Top with salmon, capers, and red onion, and serve.

3. BEET & BUCKWHEAT BLINIS WITH HORSERADISH

PREP TIME: 15 MINS · COOL TIME: 5 MINS

1 large **beet**, peeled and grated

1 tablespoon **olive oil**

2 teaspoons **caraway seeds**

juice 1 **orange**

8 **buckwheat blinis** (see page 70)

cured salmon, thinly sliced (see opposite)

1 tablespoon snipped **fresh chives**

4 **radishes**, sliced and cut into thin needles

1 × 2-inch piece of **fresh horseradish**, peeled

salt and **freshly ground black pepper**

1. Place the beet in a bowl. Heat the oil in a small pan, then add the caraway seeds and stir and cook for a minute. Add the orange juice, turn up the heat, and reduce the juice to a thick syrup. This should take a couple of minutes. Dress the beet with the syrup, season well, and let cool.

2. Top each blini with a little beet and salmon. Scatter with the chives and radishes. Finally, grate fresh horseradish over all the blinis to serve.

4. FENNEL, CELERY, & PINK PEPPERCORNS

PREP TIME: 10 MINS

cured salmon, thinly sliced (see opposite)

½ bulb of **fennel**, thinly sliced

1 **celery heart**, thinly sliced

2 teaspoons crushed **pink peppercorns**

a drizzle of **olive oil**

celery leaves

1. Arrange the salmon on a large plate and scatter with the fennel, celery, and peppercorns.

2. Drizzle with olive oil and scatter with the celery leaves to serve.

MUSSEL & ZUCCHINI FRITTERS

✓
P
SF

You can buy cooked mussel meat either fresh or frozen. Or, of course, you could cook your own.

PREP TIME: 20 MINS · STAND TIME: 20 MINS · COOK TIME: 10 MINS

1 **zucchini**, grated

½ teaspoon **salt**

½ lb cooked **mussel meat**

1 bunch of **scallions**, chopped

2 tablespoons snipped **fresh chives**

zest of 1 **lemon**

2 **eggs**

2 tablespoons **almond flour**

a pinch of **cayenne pepper**

olive oil, for frying

a bunch of **watercress**

freshly ground black pepper

RED PEPPER SAUCE

3½ oz **piquillo peppers** or peeled **red bell peppers**

1 clove of **garlic**, crushed

1 **red chile**, chopped

2 tablespoons **olive oil**

salt and **freshly ground black pepper**

1. Place the grated zucchini in a colander and sprinkle with the salt. Set aside for at least 20 minutes.

2. Place the mussel meat in a food processor and blitz for a few seconds so the mussels are coarsely chopped (this can also be done by hand). Add the mixture to a large bowl.

3. Add the rest of the ingredients to the processor and blitz briefly to combine. Empty into the bowl of mussel meat.

4. Squeeze out the liquid from the grated zucchini and add to the bowl. Fold everything together and check the seasoning.

5. Make the sauce by blending the peppers with the garlic, chile, and oil. Season to taste.

6. To cook the fritters, heat a few tablespoons of oil in a large nonstick skillet. Drop tablespoons of the mixture into the oil, pressing each one down to make a fritter about ¼ to ½ inch in thickness. Cook for 2 minutes on each side. After each batch is cooked, transfer to a plate and keep warm.

7. To serve, place a few fritters on each plate with a spoonful of the red pepper sauce and some watercress.

You could use cockles instead of the mussels . The red pepper sauce is also used on our fish soup (see page 74) and is a wonderful dip in its own right.

SQUASHED CORN CAKES

It will be very tempting to coat everything in tortilla chips after trying this recipe. These would also make a smashing breakfast patty, served with fried eggs and salsa.

PREP TIME: 25 MINS · CURE TIME: 50 MINS

1 lb 2 oz **butternut squash**, peeled and cut into small dice

2 tablespoons **olive oil**

1 **red onion**, chopped

1 clove of **garlic**, crushed

1 **red chile**, chopped

a pinch of **ground turmeric**

a pinch of **ground cumin**

3½ oz **piquillo peppers** or peeled **red bell peppers**, chopped

2 **cobs of corn**, kernels only

2 tablespoons **tomato passata**

½ cup **cannellini beans**

½ cup **kidney beans**

olive oil, for frying

avocado, lime, and cilantro salsa, to serve

salt and **freshly ground black pepper**

FOR THE COATING

¼ cup **rice flour**

2 **eggs,** beaten

1 small pack of **tortilla chips**, crushed

1. Heat the oven to 350°F.

2. Toss the squash pieces in 1 tablespoon of oil to coat then season well. Place in a roasting pan and roast in the oven for about 30 minutes, until the squash is tender. Remove from the oven.

3. While the squash is cooking, heat the remaining oil in a large skillet and cook the onion for 5 minutes over medium heat without allowing it to color. Add the garlic and spices and cook for another minute. Tip in the cooked squash along with the peppers, corn, and passata. Stir well and cook for 5 minutes.

4. Drain the beans and rinse well. Place half in a food processor and blitz for a few seconds to chop them coarsely (this can also be done by hand). Stir all the beans, chopped and unchopped, into the squash mixture, season well, then empty into a bowl and let cool.

5. Once cool, shape the mixture into 8 small cakes. Coat each one first with rice flour, then with beaten egg and finally with crushed tortilla chips. Place on a cookie sheet in the fridge to firm up (about an hour) before frying.

6. Add about ½ inch of oil to a nonstick skillet over medium-high heat. Cook the squash cakes for about 4 minutes on each side, until lightly browned. Transfer to a plate lined with paper towels to drain. Serve with avocado, lime, and cilantro salsa (see page 214), if desired.

These are great served with an avocado, lime, and cilantro salsa (see Tip on page 214).

GAJAK SNACKS

This is an assortment of Mauritian street food snacks. Perfect for a summer street party.

1. BOULETTES

These can be served in a chicken broth with chopped scallions or with hot chili sauce. You can buy chayote (they're green and look a bit like a green backside) in most African or West Indian supermarkets. They're also referred to as chowchow, so chow down.

PREP TIME: 5 MINS · COOK TIME: 20 MINS

¾ lb grated **chayote, kohlrabi,** or **daikon radish**
a pinch of **salt**
6 oz **raw shrimp**, chopped
1 tablespoon **tamari**
1 teaspoon finely grated **ginger**
3 tablespoons **tapioca starch** (approximately)
chopped **chives**, to serve

1. Place the grated chayote in a colander and sprinkle with a little salt. Let stand for 20 minutes, then place in a clean dish cloth and squeeze out any excess water.

2. Place the chayote in a bowl with the shrimp, tamari, and grated ginger. Stir in the tapioca starch a spoonful at a time, until all the ingredients are coated and the mixture comes together (this may not require the full amount called for in the ingredients list).

3. Shape the dough into balls about 1¼ inches in diameter and place in a steamer for 15 to 20 minutes. Serve scattered with chives.

2. GATEAU PIMENTS

These little hot, crispy dal fritters are sort of like falafel. Except they're not.

**PREP TIME: 10 MINS · COOK TIME: 5 MINS
SOAK TIME: OVERNIGHT**

1 cup **yellow split peas**, soaked overnight in
   lots of **cold water**
1 teaspoon **baking soda**
1 teaspoon **ground cumin**
2 tablespoons chopped **fresh cilantro**
4 **scallions**, chopped
2 **shallots**, chopped
½ teaspoon **ground turmeric**
3 **green chiles**, chopped
canola oil, for deep or shallow frying
salt and **freshly ground black pepper**

1. Drain the split peas well. Add them to a food processor with all the other ingredients except for the oil, and blitz until well combined but not completely smooth. Season.

2. Heat the oil for frying. Shape the mixture into small flattened disks and fry for a few minutes until lightly browned all over. Drain on paper towels before serving.

3. CABBAGE BHAJIS

PREP TIME: 5 MINS · COOK TIME: 8 MINS

1 cup **gram flour**

½ teaspoon **baking powder**

about ½ cup **soda water**

3 cups grated **cabbage**

1 teaspoon **ground turmeric**

a pinch of **cayenne pepper**

6 **scallions**, chopped

1 **green chile**, chopped

2 tablespoons chopped **fresh cilantro**

1 teaspoon **ground cumin**

canola oil, for frying

salt and **freshly ground black pepper**

1. Mix the flour with the baking powder and add soda water until you have a thick batter.

2. Add the rest of the ingredients, except for the oil, and mix well. The batter should just coat the cabbage. Season.

3. Heat the oil for frying, and deep-fry the bhajis at 350°F for a few minutes until browned and crisp. Drain on paper towels before serving.

ALMOND & MELON SOUP

Soaking the almonds in the water overnight gives them a better flavor. Best served totally chilled, this Spanish-inspired soup is one in a melon.

PREP TIME: 15 MINS · SOAK TIME: OVERNIGHT

1¼ cups **whole blanched almonds**

3½ cups **cold water**

3 cloves of **garlic**, crushed

3 tablespoons **sherry vinegar**

½ **cucumber**, peeled and chopped

7 oz **melon flesh** (such as cantaloupe)

⅔ cup good-quality **extra virgin olive oil**

salt and **ground white pepper**

TO SERVE

toasted almonds

a drizzle of **olive oil**

seedless **green grapes**, sliced (optional)

melon, diced (optional)

1. Soak the almonds in half the measurement water overnight.

2. Mix the almonds and 1¾ cups fresh water in a large bowl with the garlic, vinegar, cucumber, and melon. Stir to combine. Using a liquidizer, blend together in batches, adding some of the olive oil to each batch until smooth. Season well.

3. If the soup is too thick, add a little water or more olive oil to get it to the required consistency. Pass the soup through the fine blade of a food mill (mouli grater).

4. Chill the soup for at least 2 hours. Scatter with the almonds and drizzle with the oil to garnish and serve with the grapes and melon on the side, if desired. Do not try to garnish with the grapes and melon. We learned the hard way that they don't float.

> The amount of garlic can be reduced if preferred. You could also serve the soup with a few ice cubes in it if you'd like to enjoy it really chilled.

SPICED SPINACH, PEA & POTATO CAKES

Gram flour gives an epic crunch to these protein-packed patties. They work really well with the kachumber salad (see page 254) or any of the sambals from the hoppers toppers (see page 40).

PREP TIME: 5 MINS · COOK TIME: 20 MINS

2 tablespoons **gram flour**, plus extra for dusting

¼ cup cooked **spinach**

½ lb **potatoes**, mashed

⅔ cup **peas**

1 **green chile**, chopped

1 teaspoon finely grated **ginger**

2 tablespoons **cilantro**, chopped

a pinch of **ground turmeric**

a pinch of **ground cardamom**

a pinch of **garam masala**

canola oil, for frying

salt and **freshly ground black pepper**

1. Dry-fry the gram flour until lightly toasted. Place in a large bowl. Squeeze out any excess moisture from the spinach, season, and chop. Add to the gram flour along with the rest of the ingredients except for the oil. Season and mix together well.

2. Shape into small cakes and dust with a little gram flour. Shallow-fry in a little oil for 3 minutes on each side, or until lightly browned. Drain on paper towels before serving.

Serve topped with smoked or cured salmon (see page 52), or as we've done here with some cooked shrimp with a dill mayonnaise.

PUMPKIN LATKES

10½ oz **pumpkin flesh**, grated

10½ oz **cassava**, grated

½ teaspoon **salt**

6 **scallions**, chopped

½ teaspoon **ground turmeric**

1 tablespoon **mustard seeds**

1 tablespoon chopped **fresh dill**

1 **egg**, beaten

1 tablespoon **gram flour**

canola oil, for frying

freshly ground black pepper

This recipe is all about substitution. If pumpkins are not in season, use squash, or swap cassava for parsnips, taro, or sweet potatoes. When you've made these once, you'll be making them a latke.

PREP TIME: 20 MINS · COOK TIME: 10 MINS

1. Place the grated vegetables in a colander over a bowl and sprinkle with salt. Let stand for about 30 minutes. Press down with the back of a large spoon to push out any excess moisture. Transfer to a large bowl.

2. Add the rest of the ingredients except for the oil, and mix together well.

3. Heat some oil in a nonstick skillet. Drop spoonfuls of the mixture into the oil and cook for 2 minutes on each side, until golden brown and crisp. Drain on paper towels before serving.

SPICY BAKED DAL SQUARES

NF
V
Ve
SF

This spicy, savory baked lentil dish is also known as ondhwo or handvo. When Jane was at university in Leeds, she worked in an Indian restaurant called Hansa's, and this is based on a recipe she learned there.

PREP TIME: 15 MINS · FERMENTING TIME: OVERNIGHT
COOK TIME: 35 MINS

1 cup **rice flour**

1 cup **lentil/dal flour**

1 cup **warm water**

1¾ cups **coconut yogurt**

1½ teaspoons **salt**

½ teaspoon **ground turmeric**

2 **green chiles**, seeded and chopped

¾ cup **corn kernels**, cooked and chopped

1 **sweet potato**, peeled and finely chopped

2 **carrots**, grated

2 **onions**, finely chopped

2 teaspoons **baking soda**

3 tablespoons **canola oil**

1 tablespoon **black mustard seeds**

1 tablespoon **cumin seeds**

3 tablespoons chopped **fresh cilantro**

¼ cup **sesame seeds**

1. Heat the oven to 400°F.

2. Sift the rice flour and dal flour together in a large bowl. Beat in the warm water, yogurt, salt, turmeric, and chiles. Cover and let stand at room temperature overnight (about 12 hours) to ferment.

3. Add all the chopped and grated vegetables to the mixture along with the baking soda. Line a baking dish about 11 inches wide and quite deep with nonstick parchment paper and spoon the batter into the pan.

4. Heat the oil in a skillet and fry the mustard and cumin seeds until the mustard seeds pop. Stir in the cilantro and cook for 2 minutes, then spread on top of the batter in the baking pan. Sprinkle with the sesame seeds—it should resemble a crust.

5. Bake in the oven for about 30 minutes, or until a skewer comes out clean. Let cool for 30 minutes, then cut into squares and serve as an appetizer or as a side with chutneys.

SAUSAGE ROLLS

Jane's son ate the whole thing when she made these at home. For now, forget everything you think you know about lard. It's natural, unlike the polyunsaturates found in vegetable oil (but remember it works better in savory recipes). Roll with it. This pastry is particularly crumbly due to the lack of gluten, so it may be a little tricky to roll out. Don't panic if it cracks—just cover any cracks with plenty of egg wash before it goes in the oven.

PREP TIME: 20 MINS · REST TIME: 15 MINS · COOK TIME: 40 MINS

1 tablespoon **olive oil**

1 **onion**, chopped

1 **leek**, finely chopped

3 stalks of **celery**, finely chopped

1 clove of **garlic**, crushed

14 oz good-quality **sausage meat**

1 **apple**, peeled and grated

2 teaspoons **wholegrain mustard**

2 teaspoons **Dijon mustard**

2 teaspoons **Worcestershire sauce**

1 tablespoon each snipped **fresh chives** and chopped **parsley**

1 **egg**, beaten

mustard, to serve

salt and **freshly ground black pepper**

FOR THE PASTRY

1¾ cups **all-purpose gluten-free flour**, plus extra for rolling

a pinch of **salt**

3½ oz **lard**, cold and cut into chunks

1 teaspoon **modified tapioca starch** or **baking fix** (optional)

1 **egg**

1 **egg yolk**

1. Heat the oven to 400°F.

2. To make the pastry, place the flour and salt in a food processor and add the chopped lard. Add baking fix, if using (this will just help make it a bit more stretchy). Pulse to rub the fat into the flour until it resembles bread crumbs.

3. Tip out into a bowl. Beat together the egg and egg yolk and add to the flour. Bring together to a soft dough. Seal in plastic wrap and let rest in the fridge for about 15 minutes.

4. Heat the oil in a pan and cook the onions with the chopped leek and celery for about 10 minutes, until soft. Add the garlic and cook for another minute. Tip into a bowl and let cool.

5. Add the sausage meat, apple, mustards, sauce, and herbs. Season well and combine with a fork.

6. Roll out the pastry on a floured surface until approximately ¹⁄₁₆ inch in thickness. This can be done in 2 batches to make 2 rough oblongs. Work as quickly as you can, as the pastry will tend to crack. This is not a disaster, however, because you can always patch it up.

7. Place some of the sausage meat mixture in the center of each pastry oblong and brush around the edge with the beaten egg. Fold over one half of each oblong and seal the edges. Trim and brush with egg wash. Cut your large sausage into smaller sausages.

8. Place on a cookie sheet lined with nonstick parchment paper and bake for 15 minutes, then reduce the heat to 325°F and bake for another 10 minutes. Let cool and serve with mustard.

> Try swapping the sausage meat for chorizo or blood sausage (gluten- and dairy-free versions, of course). The pastry can also be used or a pie topping.

FAVA BEAN PURÉE WITH CHARD

A staple dish from Puglia, this is normally served with braised
Belgian endive but chard makes a good substitute.

PREP TIME: 10 MINS · SOAK TIME: OVERNIGHT · COOK TIME: 45 MINS

7 oz **dried split** and **peeled fava beans**, soaked overnight in plenty of **cold water**

6 cloves of **garlic**, 4 peeled and left whole, 2 crushed

⅔ cup **extra virgin olive oil**, plus extra for drizzling

7 oz **rainbow chard leaves**, stalks removed

a pinch of **dried chile flakes**

1 tablespoon **olive oil**

salt and **freshly ground black pepper**

1. Drain the beans and rinse well. Place in a large pan and cover with water. Add the whole cloves of garlic and bring to a simmer. Cook over low heat, making sure the beans are always covered with water, for about 40 minutes, or until the beans are soft. Place in a colander or sieve and let drain over the sink for about 10 minutes.

2. Transfer the beans to a food processor with the whole cloves of garlic. Add one of the crushed garlic cloves, season well, and blitz while adding the extra virgin olive oil until you have a smooth purée. You may need to add more oil. The purée should be smooth and creamy, and will thicken as it cools down. Check the seasoning.

3. Chop the chard stalks and blanch in plenty of boiling salted water for a minute. Add the leaves and cook for 30 seconds. Drain, refresh, and squeeze out any excess water. Cook the remaining crushed garlic clove and the chile flakes for a minute in the olive oil. Toss the cooked chard with the flavored oil and season well.

4. Serve the purée drizzled with a little oil, with the braised chard on the side.

 NF V SF

2½ oz **dried porcini mushrooms**

1 **onion** and 1 **leek**, finely chopped

2 tablespoons **olive oil**

1 cup **risotto rice**

1 clove of **garlic**, crushed

a splash of **vermouth** or **white wine**

up to 1¾ cups **vegetable stock**

a dash of **truffle oil**

fresh parsley and **chives**, chopped

cornstarch, to coat

2 **eggs**, beaten

polenta, to coat

canola oil, for deep frying

salt and **freshly ground black
    pepper**

PORCINI ARANCINI

Polenta makes a super substitution for traditional bread crumbs. Thank you to Hannah Bould for lending us her awesome bowls (pictured right) and having the most career-appropriate name ever.

**PREP TIME: 15 MINS · SOAK TIME: 30 MINS
COOK TIME: 45 MINS**

1. Soak the mushrooms in 1¾ cups boiling water for at least 30 minutes.

2. Cook the onion and leek in the oil for about 15 minutes over low heat without coloring. Drain the porcini, reserving the soaking liquid, and chop finely. Add the mushrooms to the vegetables along with the rice and garlic, then turn up the heat. Cook for 2 minutes, then season well and add the splash of vermouth or white wine.

3. Slowly add the porcini cooking liquid, stirring after each addition. Cook for about 20 minutes, adding some of the stock if you run out of liquid. When the rice is just cooked, remove from the heat and stir in the truffle oil and herbs. Season well and transfer to a platter or bowl. Let cool.

4. Shape the rice into balls the size of golf balls. Roll first in cornstarch, then in beaten egg, and finally in polenta. Heat the oil to 350°F and deep-fry the arancini for about 4 minutes, or until golden brown and hot in the middle. Serve scattered with extra salt.

♥ V SF

⅔ cup **almond milk**

¼ oz sachet of **active dry yeast**

1 cup **buckwheat flour**

½ cup **millet flour**

1 teaspoon **baking powder**

1 teaspoon **caraway seeds**, crushed

2 **eggs**, separated

rice bran oil, for frying

salt and **freshly ground black
    pepper**

BUCKWHEAT BLINIS

Once cooked, these will keep in the freezer for a few months for spontaneous hosting with the mosting.

**PREP TIME: 15 MINS · RISE TIME: 2 HOURS
COOK TIME: 15 MINS**

1. Warm the almond milk to tepid, whisk in the yeast, and let rest for 10 minutes.

2. Sift the flours and baking powder into a large bowl. Add the caraway seeds.

3. Beat the egg yolks into the yeast mixture and slowly add to the dry ingredients to make a thick batter. Cover and let stand for an hour to rise.

4. Whisk the egg whites until just holding. Fold into the batter and let stand for another hour. Season.

5. Heat a little oil in a nonstick skillet. Drop spoonfuls of the batter into the pan and cook for 2 minutes on each side. Drain on paper towels before serving.

ASIAN SHRIMP PANCAKES

This coconut pancake recipe is from *Everyday and Sunday: Recipes from Riverford Farm*, which Jane wrote a while ago.

PREP TIME: 15 MINS · COOK TIME: 25 MINS

FOR THE PANCAKES

1 cup **rice flour**

½ cup **gram flour**

1 large **egg**, beaten

3¼ oz **creamed coconut**, grated and mixed with 1¼ cups **boiling water**

1 teaspoon **salt**

1 teaspoon **ground turmeric**

1 teaspoon **coconut sugar**

juice of 2 **limes**

2 tablespoons **rice bran oil**

FOR THE FILLING

9 oz **raw shrimp**

1 cup **desiccated coconut**, covered in **boiling water** for 30 minutes, then excess water squeezed out

1 tablespoon chopped **fresh cilantro**

2 cloves of **garlic**, crushed

2 **red chiles**, chopped

½ cup **rice bran oil**

2 teaspoons **fish sauce**

1 tablespoon **coconut sugar**

1 teaspoon **salt**

1 teaspoon **freshly ground black pepper**

1 ripe **mango**, finely diced

1. Sift the flours together and mix with an egg in a food processor, gradually adding the creamed coconut followed by the rest of the pancake ingredients. The batter should have the consistency of light cream. Let rest for 1 hour.

2. For the filling, grind the shrimp and coconut together in a food processor.

3. Make a paste with the cilantro, garlic, and chile by pounding them together in a mortar and pestle. Cook the paste in the rice bran oil for 2 minutes. Add the shrimp and coconut and continue cooking for 10 minutes, until the shrimp are cooked. Season with the rest of the ingredients, then add the diced mango.

4. In a nonstick skillet, heat the oil and cook the pancakes in batches by dropping in a dessertspoon at a time, and spreading them out with the back of a spoon—they should have a yellow lacy appearance. Turn them over after 2 minutes to cook the other side.

5. Remove from the pan and top with a little of the mango filling to serve.

Leaves from a few sprigs of basil, mint, and cilantro can be mixed with beansprouts and served with these pancakes.

FISH SOUP

This is based on the recipe for fish soup in The Carved Angel Cookery Book by Joyce Molyneux. The soup is thickened by whisking in aïoli and gently cooking. For something a little more substantial, add chunks of firm white fish and poach them in the soup.

PREP TIME: 20 MINS · COOK TIME: 50 MINS

3 tablespoons **olive oil**

1 **onion**, chopped

½ **bulb of fennel**, chopped

½ **leek**, chopped

½ **cucumber**, chopped

1 stalk of **celery**, chopped

a pinch of **saffron**

3 sprigs of **thyme**

4 cloves of **garlic**, crushed

1 × 14 oz can of **diced tomatoes**

1 tablespoon snipped **fresh chives**

1 tablespoon chopped **fresh dill**

1 tablespoon chopped **fresh basil**

1 cup **white wine**

2 cups **fish stock**

3½ oz **smoked haddock**

juice of ½ **lemon**

salt and **freshly ground black pepper**

2 tablespoons chopped **fresh parsley**, to garnish

FOR THE AÏOLI

1 large **egg yolk** (room temperature)

2 cloves of **garlic**, crushed

⅔ cup **olive oil**

lemon juice, to taste

salt and **freshly ground black pepper**

1. Heat the oil in a large pan. Quickly blitz the vegetables in batches in a food processor so they are chopped very small but not turned to mush. Add to the pan along with the saffron and thyme. Cook for 20 minutes over low heat.

2. Add the garlic and cook for a minute. Blitz the tomatoes with the herbs and add to the vegetables. Simmer for 10 minutes until the tomatoes have reduced. Add the wine and simmer for 5 minutes, then add the fish stock. Cover and simmer for another 10 minutes, then add the fish and let poach in the stock for a further 5 minutes. Season well.

3. In a large bowl whisk the egg yolk with the garlic and slowly start to add the olive oil in a steady stream, whisking continuously until you have a thick emulsion. Season and add lemon juice to taste.

4. To serve, whisk the aïoli into the soup and heat gently, whisking until the soup thickens. Serve scattered with parsley.

We've stirred through a dollop of the red pepper sauce from page 52 here, too.

FRIED DUMPLINGS

You can substitute finely chopped shrimp, chopped mushrooms, or ground pork for the chicken. Instead of regular dumpling wrappers, these bean curd/tofu skins are wonderfully gluten-free.

PREP TIME: 20 MINS · COOK TIME: 10 MINS

1 × 1¾ oz package **bean curd/tofu skins**

rice bran oil, for shallow-frying

FOR THE FILLING

10½ oz **chicken breast**

3½ oz **mushrooms**

4 **scallions**, chopped

1 tablespoon snipped **fresh chives**

1 teaspoon **tamari**

1 teaspoon **sesame oil**

1 teaspoon **rice wine**

a pinch of **five-spice powder**

a pinch of **ground white pepper**

a thumb-sized piece of **ginger**, grated

1 teaspoon **chile paste**

½ **egg white**, whisked with 1 teaspoon **arrowroot**

1. Finely chop the chicken and mushrooms. Mix with the other ingredients, except for the tofu skins and oil for frying.

2. Separate the bean curd skins. Before using, soak each one in a little warm water to make it pliable, but for no longer than 5 to 10 seconds, or the skin will begin to cook. Place a skin on a clean cloth (this helps to stop it from sticking to your cutting board) and spread a tablespoon of shrimp mixture at one end of the oblong. Fold in the sides and roll up the skin tightly to make a long egg-roll shape. Repeat until all the filling is used.

3. Heat about ¾ inch of oil in a pan and fry the rolls, with the join underneath to prevent them from splitting, in batches, until lightly browned and crisp.

4. Serve cut in half, with a dipping sauce (see tip below).

Our favorite dipping sauce for this type of dumpling uses chiankiang vinegar, a mild and dark Chinese black vinegar. Mix 3 to 4 tablespoons of chiankiang vinegar with some grated fresh ginger and a thinly sliced clove of garlic. If you can't find the vinegar, a tamari and rice vinegar mixture will be great, too.

FOR STARTERS

TOP DIPS

Double-dipping is highly recommended. We served these with a bunch of crudités. Use whatever is in season, and serve them on a bed of crushed ice to keep them pretty and perky.

CAULIFLOWER & ANCHOVY PURÉE

PREP TIME: 5 MINS · COOK TIME: 15 MINS

1 tablespoon **olive oil**

1 **cauliflower**, cut into florets

2 cloves of **garlic**, crushed

3 **anchovies**

vegetable stock

freshly ground black pepper

1. Heat the oil in a large pan and add the cauliflower florets, garlic, and anchovies. Stir, season, and cover. Turn the heat down to very low and allow the cauliflower to steam and braise until tender.

2. Transfer to a blender, making sure all the bits of garlic and anchovy are scraped out of the pan. Add vegetable stock until you have a smooth purée, and season to taste.

1 lb 2 oz **beets**

3 tablespoons **olive oil**, plus 1 teaspoon, divided

3 tablespoons **water**

1 × ½-inch piece of **ginger**, grated

2 tablespoons chopped **fresh mint**

½ teaspoon **ground cumin**

½ clove of **garlic**, crushed

1 **avocado**

salt and **freshly ground black pepper**

FENNEL & ROSEMARY DIP

PREP TIME: 10 MINS · COOK TIME: 50 MINS

3 heads of **fennel**

2 tablespoons **olive oil**

1 clove of **garlic**, crushed

2 teaspoons chopped **fresh rosemary**

juice of ½ **lemon**

salt and **freshly ground black pepper**

1. Trim the fennel and cut into thin wedges. Heat the oil in a large pan, add the fennel, and cook over high heat for 5 minutes, or until the wedges are lightly browned.

2. Move the fennel to one side of the pan and add the garlic and rosemary. Cook for a minute, then stir them into the fennel. Season well, cover, and reduce the heat. Cook for about 30 minutes, adding water if the fennel starts to stick to the bottom of the pan.

3. When the fennel is cooked through, add the lemon juice to the mixture and purée in a blender, adding a little water if needed. Season well.

SPICED BEETS

PREP TIME: 10 MINS · COOK TIME: 50 MINS

1. Heat the oven to 325°F.

2. Clean the beets and toss them in a teaspoon of olive oil. Place in a deep roasting pan with the water, season, and cover tightly. Bake for 50 minutes, or until tender.

3. When cool enough to handle, trim and remove the skin. Cut the beets into small chunks. Add to a blender with the rest of the olive oil and all the other ingredients, and purée until smooth.

EVERYDAY EASY

GRILLED CAULIFLOWER
STEAKS WITH ROMESCO

Miss steak? Surely some mistake. These won't make you feel like you are in Texas.
They are even better than that.

PREP TIME: 20 MINS · COOK TIME: 45 MINS

1 large **cauliflower**

1 teaspoon **olive oil**

12 **scallions**

parsley leaves

FOR THE ROMESCO SAUCE

3 **tomatoes**

8 cloves of **garlic**, unpeeled

½ cup **extra virgin olive oil**

½ cup **sliced almonds**

½ cup **hazelnuts**, peeled

7 oz **piquillo peppers**

2 **red chiles**

1 teaspoon **paprika**

3 tablespoons **sherry vinegar**

salt and **freshly ground black
pepper**

1. Heat the oven to 350°F.

2. Roast the tomatoes and garlic with 1 teaspoon of the oil on a baking pan in the oven for 20 minutes. When cool enough to touch, peel the garlic and tomatoes and place the flesh in a food processor.

3. Roast the nuts in the oven for 10 minutes, until lightly browned. Let cool.

4. Add the nuts to the processor along with the peppers, chiles, and paprika. Blitz, slowly adding the rest of the oil and vinegar. Check the seasoning.

5. Place the cauliflower on a cutting board stem-side up and cut down through the core so you have 4 steaks about ¾ inch in thickness. Any excess cauliflower can be used for another dish, or for cauli-rice. Brush with olive oil and season well.

6. Trim the scallions. Heat a ridged grill pan until very hot. Place the scallions on the pan and chargrill for a minute on either side. Transfer to a plate, then cook the cauliflower steaks for 3 minutes on either side until lightly charred and tender.

7. Arrange the cauliflower steaks and scallions on a serving dish and drizzle with the romesco sauce. Serve scattered with parsley leaves.

FAVORITE FAVA FALAFEL

These are a type of Egyptian falafel, and we sphinx they rock (work with us). Made with fava beans, they are light, moist, and utterly delightful. You can by dried split fava beans online or in Asian or Middle Eastern supermarkets.

PREP TIME: 20 MINS · COOK TIME: 10 MINS
SOAK TIME: OVERNIGHT

3 tablespoons **sesame seeds**

canola, **rice bran**, or **sunflower oil**, for frying

FOR THE FALAFEL

1¾ cups **dried split fava beans** (soaked in lots of **cold water** overnight)

1 clove of **garlic**, crushed

1 **leek**, finely chopped

5 **scallions**, chopped

½ teaspoon **baking soda**

2 teaspoons **gram flour**

1 tablespoon chopped **fresh cilantro**

1 tablespoon chopped **fresh parsley**

1 teaspoon **ground cumin**

a pinch of **cayenne pepper**

salt and **freshly ground black pepper**

FOR THE MINTY TAHINI SAUCE

3 tablespoons **tahini**

½ clove of **garlic**, crushed

3 tablespoons **olive oil**

juice of ½ **lemon**

a pinch of **cayenne pepper**

salt and **freshly ground black pepper**

2 tablespoons chopped **fresh mint**

1. Drain the split fava beans well in a sieve or colander. Tip into a food processor along with the rest of the falafel ingredients. Grind to a coarse paste, and tip out onto a clean work surface.

2. Divide the mixture into 12 to 16 balls about the size of a small golf ball. Press down on them with your fingers to make small patties.

3. Sprinkle a few tablespoons of sesame seeds on a plate and coat each side of the falafels coarsely with the seeds. Let stand in the fridge for at least 10 minutes.

4. To cook the falafel, add the oil to the depth of an inch or two in a small pan over high heat. The oil will be ready when a piece of bread dropped in sizzles and turns brown quickly. Turn the heat down and start to cook the falafel in batches. We cook them four at a time and keep them warm on a baking pan in a low oven. Cook each side for 2 to 3 minutes, or until they are golden brown, then flip them over and fry the other side.

5. Beat all the ingredients for the minty tahini sauce together and thin down to pouring consistency with a little cold water. Serve.

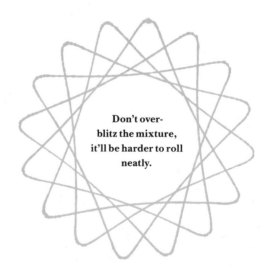

Don't over-blitz the mixture, it'll be harder to roll neatly.

NASI GORENG

This is an Indonesian staple, and it's perfect for using up leftovers. Pork, chicken, or vegetables are all welcome in this mish-mash.

PREP TIME: 15 MINS · SOAK TIME: OVERNIGHT

1 large head of **cauliflower**

4 **eggs**, beaten

1 tablespoon **rice bran oil**

2 tablespoons **dried shrimp**

4 cloves of **garlic**, crushed

2 **red chiles**, chopped

1 tablespoon **roasted peanuts**

1 × ¾-inch piece of **ginger**, grated

2 tablespoons **coconut oil**

2 **shallots**, chopped

2 **chicken breasts**, thinly sliced

7 oz **raw shrimp**

1 tablespoon **kejap manis**

1 bunch of **scallions**, chopped

salt and **freshly ground black pepper**

TO SERVE

cilantro leaves

½ **cucumber**, sliced

16 **cherry tomatoes**, halved

fried **eggs** (optional)

1. Cut the florets off of the cauliflower and blitz in a food processor until you have very small pieces resembling rice.

2. Beat the eggs and season well. Heat the rice bran oil in a large nonstick pan. Pour in a little of the egg mixture and tilt the pan so you have a thin omelet. Cook for a minute, then tip out of the pan onto a tray. Repeat until all the egg mixture is used up. Roll up the omelets and slice into ½-inch pieces.

3. Cover the dried shrimp with boiling water and set aside. Mix together the garlic, chiles, peanuts, and ginger in a mortar and pestle (or a blender) and pound to a thick paste. Drain the shrimp, reserving the soaking water, and chop finely. Add to the paste.

4. Heat the coconut oil in a large skillet and fry the paste for a minute without browning. Add the shallots and sliced chicken breast and stir-fry for about 5 minutes, stirring continuously. Add the raw shrimp and cook for a further 2 minutes. The shrimp and chicken should be firm to touch.

5. Add the cauliflower and cook over medium heat for 5 minutes, stirring well to combine. Add a little of the reserved shrimp-soaking water if the rice starts to stick to the pan.

6. Stir in the kejap manis, sliced omelet, and scallions. Check the seasoning and serve with cilantro leaves and with cucumber and tomatoes sliced on the side.

7. The nasi goreng can be topped with a fried egg, if you like.

EGGPLANT POLPETTINI

Itsy bitsy teeny weeny eggplant-y polpettini. These little meatless balls are a specialty in Puglia. They can be served fried as a snack with drinks, or as below with a tomato sauce. Omit the chiles and they're much more teeny people friendly.

PREP TIME: 25 MINS · COOK TIME: I HOUR

2 large **eggplants**, peeled

1 tablespoon **olive oil**, plus extra for frying

1 tablespoon **capers**, soaked and drained

2 tablespoons chopped **fresh basil**

1 tablespoon chopped **fresh mint**

1 tablespoon chopped **fresh parsley**

a large pinch of **wild oregano**

1 clove of **garlic**, crushed

1 **egg**, beaten

½ cup **ground almonds**

½ cup **almond flour**

3 tablespoons **fine cornmeal**

salt and **freshly ground black pepper**

TOMATO SAUCE

2 **onions**, finely chopped

10 cloves of **garlic**, crushed

2 **red chiles**, chopped (optional)

2 × 14 oz cans of **diced tomatoes**

TO SERVE

fresh basil leaves, torn, to serve

10 **black olives**, stoned and coarsely chopped

1. Cut the eggplants into ¼-inch slices, then cut each slice into small dice. Add the tablespoon of oil to a large pan over medium heat. Add the diced eggplant and stir. Fry for a minute, season, and cover. Cook over low heat for 5 minutes, or until tender, then place in a sieve and press out any excess moisture.

2. Put the diced eggplant into a large bowl and add the capers, herbs, garlic, egg, and ground almonds. Mix well and season. Place half the mixture in a food processor and pulse for 10 seconds, then spoon back into the bowl and mix with the remaining unprocessed eggplant.

3. Shape into small balls, about the size of a large walnut, and roll first in the almond flour and then in the cornmeal. Heat some oil in a large nonstick skillet and gently fry the balls for about 5 minutes, until browned all over. Remove from the pan and pour out any excess oil.

4. To make the Tomato Sauce, add the onion to the pan and cook over very low heat for 10 minutes. Add the garlic and chopped chile, cook for a further 2 minutes, then add the chopped tomatoes. Stir well and bring to a simmer, then cook gently for about 30 minutes. Return the polpettini to the pan and cook gently for 5 minutes.

5. Serve scattered with the torn basil leaves and chopped olives.

This dish could also be served with gluten-free pasta, zoodles, or thinly sliced Kentucky wonder beans (see page 134).

1 cup **split mung beans**

¼ cup **glutinous rice**

1 tablespoon **tamari**

1 tablespoon **toasted sesame oil**

½ teaspoon **baking soda**

1 cup **beansprouts**

1 clove of **garlic**, crushed

¼ lb **ground pork**, cooked

1 bunch of **scallions**, chopped

kimchi, drained and chopped
(optional)

oil, for frying

FOR THE DIPPING SAUCE

2 tablespoons **tamari**

1 tablespoon **rice vinegar**

2 teaspoons **raw honey**

1 cup **gluten-free all-purpose flour**

2 teaspoons **baking powder**

½ cup **dashi** or **fish stock**

2 **eggs**, beaten

3½ oz **smoked salmon**, finely sliced

7 oz **white cabbage**, shredded

½ **kohlrabi**, grated

1 bunch of **scallions**, chopped

rice bran oil

mayonnaise

½ cup **okonomiyaki sauce**

salt and **cayenne pepper**

OPTIONAL TOPPINGS

pickled ginger, **bonito fish flakes**,
nori, chopped **fresh chives**, **black
sesame seeds**

BINDAEDUK

When we started LEON, we always used mung beans as an example of things that you would think of negatively as being a little too worthy ("It's a bit mung beans and open-toe sandals"). These savory Korean pancakes require no sacrifice. They are as lovely as they are good for you.

**PREP TIME: 10 MINS · SOAK TIME: OVERNIGHT
COOK TIME: 25 MINS**

1. Soak the mung beans and rice in plenty of cold water for at least 8 hours. Drain, then blend with extra water to the consistency of heavy cream.

2. Mix together the dipping sauce ingredients with 1 tablespoon of water and 1 of the chopped scallions, and set aside.

3. Stir the rest of the ingredients, except for the oil, into the mung-bean batter. Heat 2 tablespoons of oil in a nonstick skillet and fry one-quarter of the mixture as a round pancake, pressing down a little. Fry for 3 minutes on each side, until golden brown. Repeat until all the mixture is used up.

4. Serve with the dipping sauce.

OKONOMIYAKI

These Japanese pancakes can be topped with lots of different sauces—the name literally means "what you like." You'll like them. Promise.

PREP TIME: 15 MINS · COOK TIME: 10 MINS

1. Sift the flour into a large bowl with the baking powder. Add the stock and the eggs and beat together to combine. Fold in the rest of the ingredients except for the oil.

2. Heat a little oil in a large nonstick skillet and pour in the batter to make a shape about ¾ inch thick. You can make smaller pancakes, or one or two large ones. Cook for 4 minutes on each side, or until the pancakes are firm to the touch.

3. Remove from the pan and drizzle with the mayo and okonomiyaki sauce. If you can't find okonomiyaki sauce then mix together ¼ cup tomato sauce, 2 tablespoons Worcestershire sauce and 2 tablespoons tamari – check the ingredients lists first though.)

4. Top with any of the suggested ingredients. If you have made one large pancake, slice it up to serve.

CASHEW SPIRALIZED ZUCCHINI WITH CHICKEN

With its incredibly creamy and cheesy taste, this basic cashew sauce makes a great béchamel replacement. Pick small zucchini as they'll be the least waterlogged and won't dilute your sauce.

PREP TIME: 15 MINS · SOAK TIME: OVERNIGHT · COOK TIME: 10 MINS

¾ cup **cashews**, soaked overnight in lots of **cold water**

1 cup **strong chicken stock**

2 cloves of **garlic**, crushed

3 tablespoons **olive oil**, divided

zest and juice of 1 **lemon**

1 cup **peas**

3½ oz **cooked chicken**, shredded

leaves from 1 bunch of **fresh basil**, shredded

1½ lb **zucchini**, spiralized or cut into long thin strips

salt and **freshly ground black pepper**

1. Heat the oven to 425°F.

2. Drain the cashew nuts and blend with the chicken stock until it is completely smooth.

3. Cook the garlic in a little olive oil and add the cashew sauce. Stir well to combine and bring to a simmer. Turn the heat down and add the lemon zest and juice, peas, chicken, and basil. Season well.

4. Toss the prepared zucchini in the rest of the olive oil and season. Place on a baking pan lined with nonstick parchment paper and put into the oven for 5 minutes. Remove and toss with the sauce to serve.

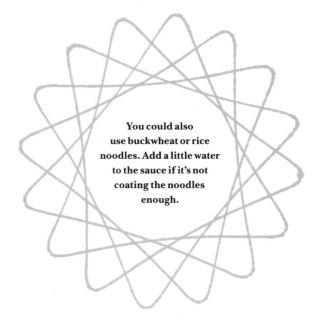

You could also use buckwheat or rice noodles. Add a little water to the sauce if it's not coating the noodles enough.

BUCKWHEAT BEET SALAD

4

This earthy, sweet, and savory salad will leave you singing Bohemian Radishy. Dry-toasting buckwheat adds an interesting texture and nutty flavor for salads.

PREP TIME: 15 MINS · COOK TIME: 5 MINS

1¼ cups **buckwheat**

2 tablespoons **caraway seeds**

7 oz **beet**, peeled and grated

2 small **carrots**, peeled and grated

juice of 1 **orange**

2 tablespoons **olive oil**

2 teaspoons **pomegranate molasses**

½ head of **radicchio**, shredded

seeds from 1 **pomegranate**

4 **radishes**, sliced

1 tablespoon chopped **fresh dill**

salt and **freshly ground black pepper**

1. Heat a nonstick skillet, add the buckwheat with the caraway seeds, and dry-roast until golden and fragrant. Remove from the heat and let cool.

2. Toss with the grated beet and carrots. Mix together the orange juice, olive oil, and pomegranate molasses and season. Drizzle half over the beet and toss together.

3. Arrange the shredded radicchio on a serving dish. Top with the beet and buckwheat. Scatter with pomegranate seeds and radish slices. Finish with chopped dill to serve.

½ cup **pecans**

2 teaspoons **olive oil**

a pinch of **cayenne pepper**

a pinch of **smoked paprika**

1 bunch of **cavolo nero**, leaves removed from central rib

1 head of **Belgian endive**, sliced

1 **apple**, thinly sliced

1 tablespoon **lemon juice**

1 **red chile**, chopped

1 **avocado**, chopped

salt

FOR THE DRESSING

3 tablespoons chopped **fresh dill**

1 tablespoon **maple syrup**

1 tablespoon **Muscatel** (or **white wine**) **vinegar**

3 tablespoons **extra virgin olive oil**

KALE, AVOCADO & APPLE SALAD

If you're looking for an extra protein fix, some pan-seared salmon would work on the side of this salad, or flaked through it.

PREP TIME: 10 MINS · COOK TIME: 6 MINS

1. Heat the oven to 350°F.

2. Toss the nuts with a little olive oil, cayenne, salt, and smoked paprika. Place on a baking pan and put into the oven for about 6 minutes, or until the nuts are lightly toasted. Let cool, then chop coarsely.

3. Shred the cavolo nero and place in a bowl with the rest of the salad ingredients. Whisk together the dressing ingredients and toss with the salad. Scatter with the chopped pecans to serve.

EVERYDAY EASY

NUTTY TURNIPS

🍴④

Turnips should not be confined to that traditional Scottish dish known as "neeps and tatties." Raw turnips give a slightly sweet, slightly mustardy flavor to this wintry salad.

PREP TIME: 10 MINS

1 **turnip**, about 14 oz, peeled

1 **apple**

2 **dried pears**, thinly sliced

⅓ cup **skinned hazelnuts**, toasted and crushed

1 tablespoon **apple cider vinegar**

2 teaspoons **wholegrain mustard**

2 tablespoons **hazelnut oil**

1 tablespoon **rice malt syrup**

2 tablespoons chopped **fresh parsley**

salt and **freshly ground black pepper**

1. Grate the peeled turnip into fine julienne. Peel the apple, chop the flesh into small dice, and mix with the turnip in a large bowl. Add the sliced dried pear and the nuts.

2. Mix together the vinegar, mustard, oil, and syrup and whisk to combine. Toss with the turnip and season well. Scatter with chopped parsley to serve.

STEAK, SOBA & SHIITAKE

Perfectly cooked steak and mushrooms. Soba hot right now.

PREP TIME: 20 MINS · MARINATE TIME: 1 HOUR · COOK TIME: 15 MINS

14 oz **sirloin steak** (or **porterhouse**)

1 clove of **garlic**, crushed

1 teaspoon **coconut sugar**

2 tablespoons **tamari**

1 tablespoon **rice vinegar**

2 teaspoons **freshly ground black pepper**

7 oz **soba noodles**

1 tablespoon **sesame oil**

2 tablespoons **rice bran oil**, divided

3 cloves of **garlic**, crushed

a pinch of **ground Sichuan pepper**

5½ oz **shiitake mushrooms**, coarsely sliced

¾ cup coarsely sliced **cremini mushrooms**

3 tablespoons **rice wine**

3 tablespoons **mirin**

1 tablespoon **tamari**

5½ oz **asparagus spears**, cut into pieces about 1 inch long

TO SERVE

watercress

6 **scallions**, chopped

cilantro leaves

1. Trim the steak into ¾-inch chunks. Stir to combine the next 5 ingredients and marinate the meat in this mixture for at least an hour.

2. Cook the soba noodles in plenty of boiling salted water for 5 minutes (or follow the directions on the package). Drain and toss in the sesame oil.

3. Heat a tablespoon of oil in a large pan and add the garlic and Sichuan pepper. Cook for a minute, then add the mushrooms. Cook over high heat for 2 minutes, then add the wine, mirin, tamari, and asparagus. Bring to a simmer and cook for 2 minutes. Fold in the soba noodles.

4. Heat the remaining tablespoon of oil until very hot in a nonstick skillet and cook the steak pieces in batches for a minute, being very careful not to overcook them. They just need to be sealed on all sides (shaking the pan will help you do this).

5. Place the noodles and watercress on a serving dish. Top with the beef and serve scattered with scallions and cilantro leaves to serve.

You can, of course, use extra cremini mushrooms if you can't find shiitake.

SWEET STUFF

The way the corn is cooked for these stuffed sweet potatoes is great on its own, too.

PREP TIME: 20 MINS · COOK TIME: 40 MINS

4 **sweet potatoes**

2 tablespoons **olive oil**

6 slices of **bacon**, chopped

1 **red onion**, chopped

1 teaspoon **fresh thyme leaves**

½ teaspoon **ground cumin**

kernels from 2 **cobs of corn**

1 **red bell pepper**, diced

2 **red chiles**, chopped

1 clove of **garlic**, crushed

3 tablespoons **white wine**

TO SERVE

1 **avocado**, chopped

juice of 1 **lime**

1 tablespoon chopped **fresh cilantro**

2 tablespoons **mayonnaise**

1 teaspoon **chipotle paste**

1. Heat the oven to 375°F.

2. Place the sweet potatoes directly on the oven shelf and bake for approximately 40 minutes, or until tender.

3. While the potatoes are baking, heat the oil in a large pan and cook the bacon for 5 minutes. Add the onion, thyme, cumin, and corn. Cook over high heat for 5 minutes to lightly brown the corn, stirring well.

4. Add the red bell pepper, chiles, and garlic. Cook for a minute, then add the wine. Stir well and cook for another 10 minutes. If the ingredients start to stick to the bottom of the pan, add a little water.

5. In a bowl, mix the chopped avocado with lime juice and cilantro. In another bowl, blend the mayonnaise with the chipotle paste.

6. Remove the sweet potatoes from the oven. Cut in half lengthwise and fluff up the flesh with a fork. Spoon some of the corn mixture onto each potato, scatter with the avocado mixture, and drizzle with the chipotle mayonnaise (make sure there's no added sugar) to serve.

These are great served as a side to barbecued or grilled steak.

TEMPEH & MUSHROOM LARB

Ground meat larb is the national dish of Laos. Here, we've made mushrooms the star of the show, with the added bonus of fermented tempeh, which is great for your health. If you're vegetarian or vegan, having to exclude recipes because of fish sauce is mightily annoying. This alternative makes 3½ fl oz but keeps well in a sealed container. Nothing fishy about that.

PREP TIME: 15 MINS · COOK TIME: 10 MINS

2 tablespoons **jasmine rice**

1 tablespoon **rice bran oil**

2 **green chiles**, chopped

1 tablespoon **lemon grass**, chopped

7 oz **tempeh**, broken into ¾-inch pieces

7 oz **shiitake mushrooms**, chopped into wedges

3½ oz **button mushrooms**, chopped into wedges

2 tablespoons chopped **fresh cilantro**

3 tablespoons chopped **fresh mint**

1 **red onion**, finely chopped

2 **Little Gem lettuces**, shredded

½ **cucumber**, cut into batons

¼ **daikon radish**, shredded

a pinch of **cayenne pepper**

FOR VEGAN FISH SAUCE

6 oz **shredded seaweed**

3 cloves of **garlic**, whole

1 teaspoon **black peppercorns**

½ cup **tamari**

½ tablespoon **miso**

FOR THE DRESSING

2 tablespoons **lime juice**

2 tablespoons **vegan fish sauce** (see above)

2 teaspoons **palm sugar**

1. Place the rice in a skillet and toast over medium heat until golden brown. Let cool, then grind to a coarse powder in a mortar and pestle or a spice grinder.

2. Heat the oil in a large pan and cook the chiles and lemon grass for 2 minutes. Add the tempeh and mushrooms. Stir-fry for 5 minutes, then tip into a bowl. Let cool a little, then stir in the chopped herbs and red onion.

3. To make the vegan fish sauce, bring the seaweed, garlic, and peppercorns to a boil with 3 cups of water. Lower the heat and let simmer for 20 minutes. Strain and return it to the pot with the tamari and cook until reduced and very salty. Remove from the heat and stir in the miso.

4. Arrange the lettuce, cucumber, and daikon radish on a serving dish. Top with the mushroom mixture. Stir together the lime, fish sauce, and sugar and drizzle it over the salad. Serve scattered with cayenne pepper and ground rice.

A squeeze of
lime juice would
be nice, too.

CAULIFLOWER & TEMPEH SAMBAL

Sambal is an Indonesian chili sauce. It's truly explosive.

PREP TIME: 15 MINS · COOK TIME: 20 MINS

1 tablespoon **rice bran oil**

3 cloves of **garlic**, crushed

1 **onion**, chopped

florets of 1 small **cauliflower**

7 oz **tempeh**, cut into thin slices

¾ cup **edamame beans**

2 **tomatoes**, skinned and chopped

1 teaspoon **tamarind paste**

1 teaspoon **palm sugar**

salt and **freshly ground black pepper**

FOR THE CHILE PASTE

4 **dried** and 4 **fresh red chiles**

1 **red onion**, chopped

1 tablespoon **capers**

2 **tomatoes**, skinned and chopped

1. Blend together the chile paste ingredients in a food processor.

2. Heat the oil in a large skillet or wok and cook the garlic and onion for a minute. Tip in the chile paste and bring up to a simmer. Cook for about 10 minutes and season well.

3. Add the vegetables, tomatoes, and ½ cup water, turn up the heat, and stir-fry for a few minutes, making sure the sauce doesn't stick to the pan. Cover and cook over low heat for 5 minutes, or until the cauliflower is just cooked.

4. Stir in the tamarind paste and palm sugar. Taste and adjust the seasoning before serving.

CAULIFLOWER TABBOULEH

Tabbouleh shan't be taboo for the gluten-free crowd.

PREP TIME: 10 MINS · COOK TIME: 3 MINS

½ small **cauliflower**, florets removed

3 tablespoons **olive oil**, divided

1 **beefsteak tomato**

leaves from 2 bunches of **fresh flat-leaf parsley**

1 bunch of **fresh mint**, leaves removed

1 bunch of **scallions**

lemon juice, to taste

a pinch of **sumac**

salt and **freshly ground black pepper**

1. Blitz the cauliflower florets in a food processor until they resemble couscous. Heat 1 tablespoon of oil in a large shallow pan. Add the cauliflower and stir-fry for a few minutes, until lightly toasted. Season well and let cool.

2. Skin and seed the tomato. Dice the tomato flesh finely. Chop the herbs and scallions.

3. Mix the tomato, herbs, and scallions with the cauliflower. Stir in the rest of the olive oil and add lemon juice to taste. Serve scattered with a pinch of sumac.

THAI FRIED-EGG SALAD

Thai the knot with this quick, punchy salad.

PREP TIME: 10 MINS · COOK TIME: 8 MINS

canola oil, for frying

4 **eggs**

2 cup **pea shoots** or **watercress**

½ **red onion**, sliced

8 **cherry tomatoes**, quartered

1 **celery heart**, thinly sliced

a handful of **beansprouts**

FOR THE DRESSING

1 clove of **garlic**, crushed

2 tablespoons **fresh cilantro stalks**
   and **leaves**, finely chopped

2 tablespoons **lime juice**

1 **red chile**, chopped

2 teaspoons **vegan fish sauce**
   (see page 102)

2 teaspoons **palm sugar**

1. Heat about ¾ inch of oil in a wok until hot. Break the eggs into ramekins and carefully tip into the oil. The eggs should puff, crackle, and crisp up. Cook for a minute on one side. Tip the eggs over for a few seconds, then remove from the oil with a slotted spoon onto a dish lined with paper towels. The eggs can be cooked one or two at a time.

2. Whisk together the dressing ingredients. Place the pea shoots (or watercress), onion, tomatoes, celery, and beansprouts in a bowl. Cut the cooked eggs into sixths and fold into the salad. Toss with the dressing and serve.

MISO HAPPY

The first time Jane made this marinated miso tofu salad, she left the cooked tofu out in the kitchen at the same time her son came home from school. It disappeared. Funny that.

PREP TIME: 20 MINS · SOAK TIME: 30 MINS · COOK TIME: 20 MINS

¼ oz **sea spaghetti** (seaweed)

9 oz **very firm tofu**

1 tablespoon **olive oil**

1 tablespoon **tamari**

1 tablespoon **arrowroot** or **cornstarch**

1 tablespoon **sesame seeds**

¾ cup **edamame beans**, cooked

2 cups **baby spinach**

¼ **cucumber**, peeled and shaved into strips

1 bunch of **scallions**, thinly sliced

6 **radishes**, thinly sliced

1 tablespoon **black sesame seeds**

FOR THE MISO WASABI SAUCE

2 teaspoons **miso paste**

1 teaspoon **wasabi paste** (or more if desired)

1 tablespoon **rice wine vinegar**

1 teaspoon **kejap manis**

1 tablespoon **grapeseed oil**

1 teaspoon **toasted sesame oil**

1. Heat the oven to 400°F.

2. Soak the sea spaghetti in lots of boiling water for at least 30 minutes. Drain and rinse well.

3. Press the block of tofu and dry with paper towels. Cut into ¾-inch cubes. In a bowl mix together the olive oil and tamari. Toss the tofu through the mixture and let stand for 15 minutes.

4. Sift the arrowroot or cornstarch over the tofu and fold through with the sesame seeds. Place on a baking pan lined with nonstick parchment paper and put into the oven for about 20 minutes, until golden brown. Give the pan a shake halfway through the cooking time.

5. While the tofu is in the oven mix together the sauce ingredients in a bowl. Remove the tofu from the oven and let cool for 10 minutes. Add to the sauce and fold through to combine.

6. In a large bowl toss the tofu and its marinade with the drained sea spaghetti and edamame beans. Arrange the spinach and cucumber on a serving dish and top with the tofu, beans, and seaweed. Scatter with the scallions, radishes, and black sesame seeds to serve.

VEGETABLE HARIRA

When people ask you how you made such a fiercely flavorful soup, tell them it's a souprise. (Sorry.) A lot of chopping goes into this soup, but if you have a food processor, let it do all the work for you. All the vegetables are interchangeable in this recipe. Just use whatever you have.

PREP TIME: 20 MINS · COOK TIME: 50 MINS
SOAK TIME: OVER NIGHT

1 cup **yellow split peas**, soaked overnight in **cold water**

2 tablespoons **olive oil**

1 **onion**, finely chopped

a pinch of **saffron**

1 × ¾-inch stick of **cinnamon**

2 **carrots**, finely chopped

2 stalks of **celery**, finely chopped

1 **leek**, finely chopped

4 **turnips**, cut into ¾-inch chunks

2 **parsnips**, cut into ¾-inch chunks

7 oz **rutabaga**, cut into ¾-inch chunks

3 cloves of **garlic**, crushed

½ teaspoon **ground turmeric**

1 teaspoon **ground coriander**

1 × 14 oz can of **diced tomatoes**

1 quart **vegetable stock**

1 × 14 oz can of **chickpeas**, drained

3 cups **spinach**

1 tablespoon chopped **fresh mint**

1 tablespoon chopped **fresh cilantro**

salt and **freshly ground black pepper**

1. Drain the yellow split peas and place in a pan. Cover with water and bring to a boil, then turn down the heat and simmer for 20 to 30 minutes, while you get started cooking the vegetables.

2. Heat the oil in a large pan and add the onion, saffron, cinnamon, carrots, celery, and leeks. Cook for about 15 minutes over low heat, without browning.

3. Add the turnips, parsnips, and rutabaga to the pan along with the garlic and spices. Drain the split peas and add them to the vegetables along with the canned tomatoes and stock. Bring to a boil, then lower the heat and simmer for 30 minutes, or until the split peas are tender. Scoop out a couple of ladlefuls and blend until smooth, either with a hand-held stick blender or in a food processor. Return this to the pan and stir into the rest of the soup.

4. Add the chickpeas and spinach and stir into the soup. Cook for another 5 minutes, adding water to thin down if necessary, then season.

5. Add a little more stock if the soup or water is too thick and serve scattered with chopped mint and cilantro.

Always give saffron a bash in a mortar and pestle, or crumble it between your fingers first. It is more expensive per gram than gold, so do omit it if it's too pricey. However, if you are going to commit, look for Persian saffron. It may cost more, but it's the best quality.

SO MANY SOBA NOODLES

The two noodle dressings here go well with soba either hot or cold. They can also be used with spiralized sweet potatoes or other vegetables. The avocado sauce is a revelation.

COOK TIME: 5 MINS

9 oz **soba noodles**

1 teaspoon **canola oil**

1. Cook the noodles in lots of boiling salted water for 5 minutes. Drain and toss in a little oil. See below for sauces to serve.

SESAME PEANUT SAUCE

PREP TIME: 10 MINS

¼ cup **toasted sesame seeds**

1 × 1¼-inch piece of **ginger**, finely grated

2 cloves of **garlic**, crushed

4 **scallions**, chopped

¾ cup **smooth peanut butter**

3 tablespoons **tamari**

2 tablespoons **rice vinegar**

1 tablespoon **brown rice syrup**

2 teaspoons **chile paste**

½ teaspoon **Sichuan peppercorns**, crushed

2 tablespoons **sesame oil**

¾ cup **water**

TO GARNISH

extra **toasted sesame seeds**

scallions, chopped

1. Blend all the ingredients together until smooth.

2. Toss the cooked noodles with the sauce. The noodles can be enjoyed either hot or chilled, scattered with sesame seeds and scallions.

AVOCADO SAUCE

PREP TIME: 10 MINS

2 **avocados**, chopped

juice of ½ **lemon**

1 clove of **garlic**, crushed

3 tablespoons **olive oil**, plus extra if needed

2 **red chiles**, chopped

2 tablespoons chopped **fresh parsley**

salt and **freshly ground black pepper**

1. Place the avocados in a blender with the lemon juice, garlic, and olive oil.

2. Season well, adding a little water if needed so that the sauce has a coating consistency.

3. Toss the cooked noodles in the avocado sauce and scatter with the chopped chiles and parsley.

FRIDGE SOUP

This is a soup designed to use up all those leftover salad greens and vegetables that generally end up being thrown out, or don't look too special since they are particularly perishable.

PREP TIME: 10 MINS · COOK TIME: 25 MINS

2 tablespoons **olive oil**

1 **onion**, sliced

2 cloves of **garlic**, crushed

any herbs, such as **fresh basil**, **tarragon**, or **chives**, chopped

¼ **cucumber**, sliced

4 **scallions** or 1 **leek**, chopped

2 **potatoes**, peeled and thinly sliced

3½ oz **mixed lettuce leaves** or 1 head of **lettuce**

3½ cups **vegetable** or **chicken stock**

snipped **fresh chives**

a pinch of **ground nutmeg**

salt and **freshly ground black pepper**

1. Heat the oil in a large pan and add the onion. Cook for 5 minutes, then add the garlic, herbs, cucumber, scallions, and sliced potatoes. Season well and cook for another 10 minutes, stirring to prevent the vegetables from sticking.

2. Add the lettuce to the pan, tearing up any large leaves, and add the stock. Bring to a boil, then reduce the heat and simmer for 10 minutes, or until the potatoes are tender.

3. Blend the soup until smooth and check the seasoning, adding extra stock if the soup is too thick. For a very smooth result pass the soup through the finest setting of a food mill (mouli grater).

4. Serve with chopped chives and a little ground nutmeg.

This ingredient list is a guide, but you can use anything like radishes, cabbage, or broccoli. When in season, ramsons would make a great addition.

MUSHROOM BUN BURGERS

✓
P
NF
SF

Who needs burger buns? One for the carnivores out there because the meaty consistency and taste of the meadow mushrooms is flipping fantastic. Do make sure you have plenty of paper towels on hand. These bad boys are so juicy that "drippage" is unavoidable.

PREP TIME: 15 MINS · COOK TIME: 25 MINS

1¼ lb **ground veal** (or **pork**)

1 tablespoon chopped **fresh parsley**

1 tablespoon chopped **fresh chives**

zest of ½ **lemon**

1 clove of **garlic**, crushed

a dash of **chili sauce**

2 **egg yolks**

8 large flat **meadow mushrooms**

2 tablespoons **olive oil**, divided

1 **red onion**, sliced

4 **gherkins**, sliced

3½ oz **baby salad leaves**

salt and **freshly ground black pepper**

1. Heat the oven to 325°F.

2. Mix the ground meat with the herbs, lemon, garlic, chili sauce, and egg yolks. Season well and mix together. Shape into 4 patties and let chill in the fridge for a few hours.

3. Brush the mushrooms with 1 tablespoon of the oil and season. Bake in the oven for 15 minutes, until just tender.

4. Take the burgers out of the fridge 30 minutes before cooking. Heat a griddle and brush the burgers with the remaining oil. Griddle for 4 minutes on each side. Let rest for a few minutes. Sandwich each burger between 2 mushrooms. Top with onion and gherkin slices. Serve with a green salad.

Veal is a lean, versatile meat that contains less fat than beef, and is rich in protein, zinc, niacin, and vitamins B$_{12}$ and B$_6$.

TEA LEAF SALAD

Rather than Great Britain's traditional cup of tea, this fermented tea leaf salad is a national favorite in Myanmar. Crunchy, sweet, sour, and savory, it's a daily dish for the whole country, especially students, who like it for its caffeine buzz. We're into it.

PREP TIME: 15 MINS · COOK TIME: 5 MINS · SOAK TIME: OVER NIGHT

3 tablespoons **split yellow peas**, soaked overnight

2 tablespoons **rice bran oil**

8 cloves of **garlic**, thinly sliced

3 tablespoons **fermented tea leaves**

1 tablespoon **dried shrimp**, chopped

1 **beefsteak tomato**, chopped

3½ cups **cabbage**, very thinly sliced

2 tablespoons **roasted peanuts**

2 tablespoons **toasted sunflower seeds**

1 tablespoon **toasted sesame seeds**

1 tablespoon **lime juice**

1 **red chile**, chopped

1 teaspoon **tamari**

TO SERVE
lime wedges (optional)
fresh cilantro (optional)

1. Drain the split peas and fry in a tablespoon of the oil until lightly toasted. Remove from the pan and set aside. Heat the remaining oil in the pan, and fry the garlic slices until lightly browned.

2. Mix the split peas and garlic with the rest of the ingredients. Toss together and serve with lime wedges and cilantro leaves, if desired.

SPROUTED BUCKWHEAT & SPROUT SALAD WITH SMOKED TROUT

Jane thought it would be funny to put something sprouted with sprouts. Sprouting the buckwheat does take a little love and attention, but is a great science experiment for the little ones.

PREP TIME: 10 MINS · SOAK TIME: 2 DAYS

½ cup **buckwheat**

juice of ½ **lemon**

3 tablespoons **olive oil**

2 teaspoons **maple syrup**

1 teaspoon **English mustard**

3½ oz **Brussels sprouts**, shredded

2 cups **baby spinach**

2 tablespoons chopped **fresh dill** (or **chives**)

2 tablespoons chopped **fresh mint**

14 oz **smoked trout** (or **cooked trout/salmon**)

handful of **wild garlic flowers**, to garnish (optional)

salt and **freshly ground black pepper**

1. Rinse the buckwheat well in lots of cold running water. Add to a bowl, cover with water, and let soak for about an hour. Drain, then spread the buckwheat in a fine sieve over a bowl. Cover with a clean damp cloth and let stand at room temperature, rinsing the buckwheat twice a day with water until sprouts start to appear. Transfer to the fridge.

2. Whisk together the lemon juice, oil, maple syrup, and mustard to make the dressing and season well.

3. In a large bowl mix the buckwheat with the sprouts, spinach, and herbs. Toss with the dressing. Pull apart the smoked trout into 1-inch pieces and fold into the salad. Garnish with wild garlic flowers (if using) to serve.

SPEEDY SUPPERS

COCONUT WATER FRIED CHICKEN

This is a grown-up version of fried chicken.
The coconut water adds a delicacy to the dish that your guests will go nuts for.

PREP TIME: 30 MINS · COOK TIME: 15 MINS
MARINATING TIME: OVERNIGHT

1¾ cups **coconut water**

1 clove of **garlic**, crushed

3 **shallots**, chopped

1 × ¾-inch cube of **ginger**,
   grated finely

2 **red chiles**, chopped

½ teaspoon **ground turmeric**

1 teaspoon **ground coriander**

1 teaspoon **salt**

8 to 10 **chicken thighs**
   (about 2¾ lb)

canola oil (or **vegetable oil**),
   for frying

½ cup **rice flour**

½ cup **cornstarch**

sprigs of **cilantro**, to serve

½ a **lime**, to serve

1. Coarsely blend the coconut water with the garlic, shallots, ginger, chiles, and spices. Place the chicken in a shallow container and add the coconut spice mixture. Massage the mixture onto the chicken with your hands to coat well. Cover and let marinate overnight.

2. Place the chicken and its marinade in a large pan. Bring to a boil, then simmer over low heat for about 20 minutes. Turn off the heat and let the chicken cool down in the marinade. At this point the chicken can sit in the fridge, still in the marinade, until needed.

3. Heat about 2 inches of oil in a pan until it's approximately 350°F, or until a piece of bread dropped into the oil turns brown.

4. Sift together the 2 flours and tip them onto a platter or plate. Remove the chicken from the marinade and toss it in the flour. Gently lower into the hot oil with a slotted spoon and fry for about 10 to 15 minutes over medium heat, until golden brown. It is best to do 3 or 4 thighs at a time. Overcrowding the pan will cause the temperature of the oil to drop, with the result that the chicken will stew in the oil. Remove the fried chicken from the oil with a slotted spoon and place on a plate lined with paper towels to drain. Keep the cooked chicken warm while you fry the rest of the chicken. Serve with cilantro and a squeeze of lime.

**Any leftover
marinade makes a great
base for a spicy chicken
noodle soup.**

LEON'S GFC
(Gluten-free Fried Chicken)

In the LEON development kitchen, we have spent a long time trying to perfect our gluten-free fried chicken. We think we've finally nailed it with this tempura-style batter, which doesn't compromise on crunch. The colder the fizzy water, the better. Batter than the dirty version.

PREP TIME: 10 MINS · COOK TIME: 10 MINS

6 **boneless chicken thighs**, cut into small dice or strips

oil, for frying

FOR THE BATTER

½ cup **cornstarch**

½ cup **gram flour** (or other **GF flour**)

1 **egg yolk**

¾ cup **sparkling water**

2 tablespoons **ground almonds**

1 tablespoon **mustard powder**

1 tablespoon **dried oregano**

1 tablespoon **chili powder**

½ tablespoon **onion powder**

½ tablespoon **salt**

½ tablespoon **freshly ground black pepper**

mayonnaise and coarsely chopped **tarragon**, to serve

1. Vigorously beat the flours, egg yolk, sparkling water, ground almonds, and mustard powder together, then stir in the spices and seasoning.

2. Coat the chicken in the batter and shallow-fry for 5 minutes, turning halfway, until golden and cooked through.

3. Place on a plate lined with paper towels to soak up excess oil, season to taste, and serve with mayonnaise (check that there's no added sugar) mixed with tarragon for dipping.

For a change, try adding the spices to oats or gluten-free cornflakes instead of making the batter.

CHICKEN, LEMON & OLIVE TAGINE

This recipe, developed by Kay Plunkett-Hogge, has been the most popular seasonal stew on the LEON menu in years. It's summer in a stew.

PREP TIME: 15 MINS · MARINATING TIME: 1 HOUR · COOK TIME: 1 HOUR

1 lb 2 oz **chicken thighs**, skinless and boneless, cut into ¾-inch cubes

¼ teaspoon **ground ginger**

½ teaspoon **freshly ground black pepper**

1 stick of **cinnamon**

a good pinch of **saffron**

2 teaspoons **ground cumin**

½ teaspoon **ground turmeric**

1 teaspoon **ras el hanout**

3 tablespoons **olive oil**

1 **onion**, peeled and chopped

3 cloves of **garlic**, crushed

1 cup **chicken stock**

1 tablespoon **preserved lemon brine**

1 cup **pitted green olives**

1 **preserved lemon**, seeded and chopped

¼ cup chopped **fresh parsley**, to serve

salt and **freshly ground black pepper**

1. Marinate the chicken with the dry spices and 1 tablespoon of olive oil for an hour.

2. Cook the onion and garlic in the remaining olive oil until just soft and turning golden.

3. Add the chicken and stir until combined. Add the stock and the preserved lemon brine, bring to a boil, then let simmer, covered, for 35 minutes.

4. Now add the olives and preserved lemon, and taste for seasoning. Let simmer for a further 5 minutes. Remove the chicken and olives and cook the sauce for a further 3 to 5 minutes to reduce. Shred the chicken cubes into strips.

5. Return the chicken to the sauce very briefly to bring everything together, then serve with a parsley garnish.

Add chickpeas to bulk out the chicken if you're on a budget. We like to serve this in our restaurants on a bed of brown rice with a wedge of fresh lemon.

TURKEY SAN CHOY BAU

These little Chinese lettuce parcels are such an easy one-pot supper. We've used turkey here because it's lean, but you can use chicken, pork, or tofu instead, if you prefer.

PREP TIME: 15 MINS · COOK TIME: 10 MINS

1 tablespoon **rice bran oil**

1 clove of **garlic**, crushed

1 × ¾-inch piece of **ginger**, finely grated

10½ oz **turkey breast**, chopped

3½ oz **shiitake mushrooms**, chopped

4 **water chestnuts**, cut into thin needles

2 teaspoons **Sichuan peppercorns**, crushed

2 tablespoons **tamari**, plus extra to serve

6 **scallions**, chopped, divided

1¾ oz **rice noodles** (optional)

oil, for deep frying (optional)

salt and **freshly ground black pepper**

TO SERVE

3 **Little Gem** or 1 **iceberg lettuce**

½ **cucumber**, seeded and thinly sliced

sugar-free chili sauce (optional)

a handful of **beansprouts**

1. Heat the oil in a wok or skillet. Add the garlic, ginger, and turkey and stir-fry for 3 minutes. Add the mushrooms, water chestnuts, peppercorns, and tamari. Cook for another 2 to 3 minutes, then season and add half the scallions. Set aside.

2. If using the noodles, heat the oil to 350°F and fry them until crisp. Drain on paper towels.

3. Break up the noodles and mix with the turkey and mushroom mixture and the rest of the scallions. Transfer to a serving dish.

4. Serve with the lettuce leaves, cucumber, tamari and chili sauce, if using. A fun one for little hands to make their own parcels.

SALT-N-PEPA SQUID

Push it, push it real good.

PREP TIME: 15 MINS · COOK TIME: 15 MINS

cornstarch, to coat

flaxseed oil, for deep-frying

7 oz **green snap beans** and **Kentucky wonder beans**, trimmed

7 oz **squid pieces** and tentacles, cleaned

1 tablespoon **canola oil**

4 cloves of **garlic**, thinly sliced

2 **red chiles**, sliced

4 **scallions**, sliced

salt and **freshly ground black pepper**

FOR THE BATTER

2 tablespoons **potato starch**

2 tablespoons **tapioca flour**

2 tablespoons **arrowroot**

1 teaspoon **Sichuan peppercorns**, ground

a large pinch of **salt**

about 3½ fl oz **soda water**

a pinch of **baking soda**

1. Sift together the potato starch, tapioca, and arrowroot. Stir in the salt and pepper. Whisk in the soda water until you have a thin batter, then add a large pinch of baking soda.

2. Pour a few tablespoons of cornstarch onto a plate and season.

3. Heat the oil for deep-frying to about 350°F. You will need to deep-fry the beans and squid in batches. First toss them in the cornstarch, then quickly dredge in the batter and fry for a few minutes until crisp.

4. While the beans and squid are frying, heat the tablespoon of flaxseed oil in a nonstick skillet and cook the garlic and chile for a few minutes, until the garlic is golden brown. Add the scallions at the last minute and toss together. Drain on paper towels.

5. When all the beans and squid have been cooked, serve on a dish scattered with the garlic, chiles, and scallions.

Use flaxseed oil instead of canola oil if you want to make this paleo.

RUNNER BEAN PASTA

In Puglia, Jane went to a farmhouse near Ostuni called Il Frantoio. The food there is all very vegetable based and they serve a dish using "fagiolini di mezzometro" or "half-meter beans," where the beans are dressed with a tomato sauce and look very much like a thick pasta. No need run away from home and escape to Puglia. We've brought the recipe to you.

PREP TIME: 10 MINS · COOK TIME: 2 TO 3 MINS

1 lb 2 oz **runner beans** or **Kentucky wonder beans**, trimmed and cut into thin long strips

1. Trim the beans and slice into long thin strips. A bean slicer will do this for you (or recruit someone to slice the beans for you).

2. Cook in lots of boiling salted water for 2 minutes. Drain and toss with one of the following sauces to serve.

VONGOLE

PREP TIME: 10 MINS · COOK TIME: 10 MINS

2¼ lb **clams**
½ cup **white wine**
3 cloves of **garlic**, 1 crushed and 2 chopped
2 tablespoons **olive oil**
2 **red chiles**, chopped
2 tablespoons chopped **fresh parsley**
extra virgin olive oil

1. Heat a large pan until very hot. Add the clams along with the wine and crushed garlic. Shake the pan, cover, and let cook for 2 to 3 minutes, or until the clams have started to open. Drain the clams in a colander over a bowl to collect the cooking liquor.

2. Heat the oil in a large pan and add the chopped garlic and chile. Cook for a minute, then add the clam cooking liquor. Cook over high heat until it has reduced enough to coat the back of your wooden spoon.

3. Add the cooked beans to the pan along with the cooked clams. Toss together with the chopped parsley and serve drizzled with olive oil.

SALT COD, TOMATO & PARSLEY

PREP TIME: 10 MINS · COOK TIME: 5 MINS

2 tablespoons **olive oil**
1 clove of **garlic**, crushed
1 **red chile**, finely chopped
4 **anchovy fillets**
15 **cherry tomatoes**, quartered
2 tablespoons chopped **fresh parsley**
7 oz **cooked salt cod**, flaked
a drizzle of **extra virgin olive oil**
salt and **freshly ground black pepper**

1. Heat the olive oil in a large pan. Add the garlic and chile and cook over medium heat for a minute, being careful not to color the garlic. Take off the heat and add the anchovies, beating vigorously until they "melt" into the oil.

2. Drain the cooked beans and add to the anchovy and chile oil, tossing until the beans are well coated.

3. Fold in the tomatoes, parsley, and salt cod and season well. Serve drizzled with good extra virgin olive oil.

CARBONARA

When making Carbonara sauce, just use the prepared beans raw. They will cook in the sauce.

PREP TIME: 10 MINS · COOK TIME: 15 MINS

2 tablespoons **olive oil**

4 cloves of **garlic**

7 oz **pancetta lardons** (or **sliced pancetta**)

2 **eggs**

1 **egg yolk**

1 tablespoon chopped **fresh parsley**

1 tablespoon snipped **fresh chives**

salt and **freshly ground black pepper**

1. Heat the oil in a skillet and gently cook the garlic for 3 minutes over medium heat until the garlic starts to turn brown. Remove from the pan and add the pancetta. Cook for about 5 minutes, until the pancetta is golden.

2. Whisk the eggs and yolk together.

3. Bring a large pan of well salted water to a boil. Drop in your (raw) runner beans and cook for about 3 minutes, or until the beans are tender. Drain and reserve a couple of tablespoons of cooking water.

4. Add a tablespoon of the cooking water to the eggs and beat together. Return the runner beans to the pan while still hot. Add the pancetta, along with the fat. Stir well and add the egg mixture. Make sure the pan is off the heat (you don't want scrambled eggs) and fold through until all the bean strips are coated. Season well with black pepper and serve topped with the herbs.

If the sauce seems too dry, add some extra cooking water until it is the desired consistency.

MUSSEL & SMOKED SALMON

PREP TIME: 10 MINS
COOK TIME: 15 MINS

1 lb 2 oz **mussels**, cleaned

2 cloves of **garlic**, crushed

½ cup **white wine**

1 tablespoon **olive oil**

1 tablespoon chopped **fresh rosemary**

1 **red bell pepper**, finely diced

3½ oz **smoked salmon**, chopped

1. Heat a pan until very hot. Tip in the mussels with the garlic and white wine, give the pan a shake, and cover. Cook for 2 to 3 minutes, or until the mussels have just opened. Pour the mussels into a colander over a bowl, to collect the cooking liquor.

2. Heat the oil in a pan and cook the rosemary with the red bell pepper for about 5 minutes. Add the mussel liquor and reduce by half.

3. While the sauce is reducing, pick the mussels from the shells. Add the mussels along with the chopped smoked salmon to the reduced sauce and toss with the cooked runner beans or Kentucky wonder beans.

EGGPLANT, TOMATO, OLIVE & BASIL

PREP TIME: 10 MINS
COOK TIME: 50 MINS

2 **eggplants**

3 tablespoons **olive oil**

5 cloves of **garlic**, finely sliced

a pinch of **chile flakes**

1 × 14 oz can of **diced tomatoes**

2 teaspoons **balsamic vinegar**

1 tablespoon **black olives**, chopped

1 tablespoon **capers**

2 tablespoons shredded **fresh basil**

a drizzle of **extra virgin olive oil**

salt and **freshly ground black pepper**

1. Chop the eggplant into ¾-inch chunks. Heat the olive oil in a large pan and brown the eggplant in batches, cooking each batch for about 5 minutes. Don't cook them all at once, or they won't brown.

2. Remove from the pan with a slotted spoon and let drain on a plate lined with paper towels.

3. Add the garlic and chile flakes to the pan. Cook for a minute, then add the canned tomatoes. Simmer the sauce for about 20 to 30 minutes, or until it has reduced. Add the vinegar and return the browned eggplant chunks to the pan. Cook for 10 minutes over low heat.

4. Add the olives, capers, and basil. Check the seasoning and toss with the cooked beans. Drizzle with good extra virgin olive oil to serve.

BLACK & WHITE SQUID

This visually stunning stir-fry is tender, while retaining lots of satisfying crunch. The trick with squid is to cook it very, very quickly. This isn't a dish to turn your back on.

PREP TIME: 30 MINS · COOK TIME: 7 MINS

1¼ lb **squid**, cleaned

1 head of **fennel**

1 **red onion**, thinly sliced

2 **zucchini**

1 **red bell pepper**

3½ oz **runner beans** or **Kentucky wonder beans**

2 tablespoons **olive oil**

1 package of **squid ink**

2 **red chiles**, finely chopped

2 tablespoons chopped **fresh flat-leaf parsley**

1 clove of **garlic**, crushed

3 tablespoons **extra virgin olive oil**

salt and **freshly ground black pepper**

1. Slice the squid bodies into long thin strips. Cut the tentacles into similar-size pieces. Set aside.

2. Slice all the vegetables into long thin strips of similar size. Heat a tablespoon of olive oil in a large skillet or wok until very hot. Tip in the vegetables and fry quickly for a few minutes, until just cooked. Season well and transfer to a serving platter.

3. Heat the remaining oil in the pan until very hot. Add half the squid and cook for about 30 seconds, stirring well. Season and remove from the pan to another dish using a slotted spoon. While the pan is still hot, add the other half of the squid and fry quickly for a few seconds, then add the squid ink. Cook for about 20 seconds, so the squid is coated and hot.

4. Spoon the black squid onto the vegetables and set the white squid on top.

5. Mix the chiles, parsley, and garlic with the extra virgin olive oil and drizzle the mixture over the squid to serve.

✓
♥
NF
V
Ve
SF

BRAZILIAN BLACK BEAN STEW

Our version of the traditional Brazilian feijoada. It tastes decadent while being remarkably good for you. It's so hearty and filling that when Adam, John's best friend and our property director at LEON, first tried this new vegan dish, he said, "I love that new meaty one."

PREP TIME: 15 MINS · COOK TIME: 40 MINS

1 large **onion**, coarsely chopped

2 tablespoons **canola oil**

1 **carrot**, chopped into disks

1 stalk of **celery**, chopped

½ **leek**, chopped

1 **bay leaf**

1 teaspoon **tomato paste**

1 teaspoon **sweet paprika**

½ teaspoon **smoked paprika**

1 teaspoon **chipotle sauce**

1 teaspoon **dried oregano**

2 cups cooked **black beans**

1¼ cups **vegetable stock**

1 clove of **garlic**, crushed

1 tablespoon **tamari**

1 teaspoon **red wine vinegar**

salt and **freshly ground black pepper**

1 tablespoon chopped **fresh cilantro**

1. In a large pan, cook the onion in the oil for 5 minutes over medium heat. Add the carrot, celery, leek, and bay leaf. Stir well and cook gently for about 20 minutes, without browning the vegetables.

2. Add the tomato paste, spices, and herbs and cook for another 5 minutes, stirring well to combine.

3. Add the beans, stock, garlic, tamari, and vinegar. Turn up the heat and cook until the sauce has thickened to coat the beans and vegetables. Season well and serve sprinkled with cilantro.

We serve our stew with brown rice and a little fresh cilantro scattered on top.

FISH FINGERS WITH
A SESAME COCONUT CRUST

Consider these to be a kind of fancy fish fingers. Any firm white fish works well, like gurnard, bream, or bass. Another one bites the crust.

PREP TIME: 10 MINS · COOK TIME: 10 MINS

4 × 5½ oz **firm white fish fillets**, skinned

2 teaspoons **wasabi paste**

3 tablespoons **rice bran oil**

a squeeze of **lime juice**, to serve

wilted spinach or **rainbow chard**, to serve

salt and **cayenne pepper**

FOR THE PASTE

1 teaspoon **palm sugar**

1 **egg**, beaten

1 tablespoon **tamari**

3 tablespoons **sesame seeds**

2 tablespoons **desiccated coconut**

2 tablespoons chopped **fresh cilantro**

1 clove of **garlic**, crushed

1. Heat the oven to 300°F.

2. Mix the paste ingredients together in a bowl and set aside.

3. Season the fish well and let stand for 15 minutes. Dry with paper towels then spread a little wasabi on one side of each fillet. Press the paste onto each fillet, on top of the wasabi.

4. Heat the oil in an ovenproof skillet. Gently fry the fish fillets, paste-side down, for 3 minutes or until the crust is browned. Carefully flip them over and transfer the pan to the oven. Cook for about 5 minutes. The cooking time may vary depending on the thickness and type of fish used.

5. Serve with wilted spinach or rainbow chard and a squeeze of lime.

Serve with braised kale, spinach, or lentils. If you're not a fan of fish, the crust works just as well on chicken.

LAMB & ROASTED
SUMMER VEGETABLES

Jane ate this very simple dish at Trattoria La Madia in Lombardy. A friend of hers, Christine Smallwood, was there to interview the chef for her book about the region. Jane was there to crash a bunch of photoshoots while on a camping trip. Roasting vegetables is not just for winter roots—any type can be used, but just add the vegetables that take less time to cook 5 minutes before serving.

PREP TIME: 20 MINS · COOK TIME: 40 MINS

1 lb 2 oz **mixed vegetables** (to include **cauliflower**, **romanesco**, **radishes**, **fennel**, **zucchini**, **turnips**, **baby carrots**, **green snap beans**, **peas**, and **cabbage**)

3 tablespoons **olive oil**

2 cloves of **garlic**, crushed

3 tablespoons chopped **fresh herbs** (**chives**, **tarragon**, and **chervil**)

10½ oz **lamb loin** or **lamb leg steaks**, trimmed

salt and **freshly ground black pepper**

1. Heat the oven to 350°F.

2. Cut the cauliflower and romanesco into small florets, halve the radishes, slice the fennel, and chop the zucchini and turnips. Toss in olive oil with the garlic and herbs. Place on a baking pan and put into the oven. Roast for about 25 minutes, giving them a stir after 15 minutes.

3. Meanwhile cut the rest of the vegetables (except the peas and cabbage) into small pieces. Add them all to the pan and cook for another 5 minutes.

4. While the vegetables are cooking, season the lamb loins or steaks and pan-fry in a little olive oil for about 6 minutes, turning frequently until slightly firm to touch. Let rest for at least 5 minutes.

5. Slice the lamb thinly and fold into the vegetables before serving.

SOLE & GRAPE SALAD

A salad so light and fresh it gives you grape expectations for a long, hot summer.

PREP TIME: 15 MINS · COOK TIME: 5 MINS

10½ oz **flounder fillets**, skinned

1 teaspoon **cayenne pepper**

½ cup **grapes** (peeled if you have the time)

2 **shallots**, sliced

leaves from a small bunch of **fresh tarragon**

10 **radishes**, quartered

¼ **cucumber**, peeled, seeded, and cut into thin slices

2½ oz **corn salad**

FOR THE DRESSING

¼ cup **white grapes**

2 tablespoons **moscatel vinegar**

¼ cup **grapeseed oil**

salt and **freshly ground black pepper**

1. Trim the fish fillets. Place on a plate and sprinkle with about ½ teaspoon of salt. Cover and place in the fridge.

2. Cut the grapes in half and mix with the shallots, tarragon, radishes, and cucumber.

3. Make the dressing by blending all the ingredients together, then passing through a sieve. Season well.

4. Take the fish out of the fridge and dry with paper towels. Place on a clean plate and sprinkle with cayenne. Put the plate in a steamer and steam for about 5 minutes, or until the fish is just firm.

5. Arrange the grapes, shallots, cucumber, radishes, and herbs on a plate with the corn salad. Top with the sole fillets and drizzle with the dressing to serve.

To skin your grapes easily, cover them with boiling water and let stand for a few minutes, then drain and peel.

JERK PORK

Don't be a jerk, make a jerk. Serve it in a corn tortilla or flatbread (pages 248 and 250).

PREP TIME: 15 MINS · MARINATING TIME: OVER NIGHT · COOK TIME: 10 MINS

2¾ lb **pork fillet**

corn tortillas (see page 248),
   to serve

FOR THE MARINADE

6 **red chiles**, finely chopped

3 cloves of **garlic**, crushed

1 bunch of **scallions**, chopped

1 × 1¼-inch piece of **ginger**, finely
   grated

2 tablespoons **sambal oelek**, or
   make your own (see hoppers
   toppers, page 40)

3 tablespoons **rice bran oil**

2 tablespoons **rice vinegar**

1 teaspoon **ground allspice**

3 tablespoons **tamari**

salt and **freshly ground black
   pepper**

FOR THE PINEAPPLE SALSA

½ **pineapple**, peeled and cut into
   small dice

1 **red chile**, seeded and finely
   chopped

1 tablespoon **cilantro**, chopped

juice of 1 **lime**

salt and **freshly ground black
   pepper**

1. Trim the pork fillet, removing any sinew, and slice the meat diagonally across into pieces ¾ inch in thickness.

2. Put all the marinade ingredients into a food processor and blend until smooth. Place in a container with the meat and rub the marinade into the pork using your fingers. If time allows, let the pork marinate overnight in the refrigerator.

3. Mix all the ingredients for the pineapple salsa together, season, and set aside.

4. Heat a heavy, ridged grill pan (or a barbecue) until very hot. Grill the pork fillet pieces for 2 minutes on each side, until almost firm to the touch. The pork can be served slightly pink. This can be done in batches, with the cooked pork held in a warm dish until ready to serve.

5. Any remaining marinade can be simmered with a little water for 10 minutes and poured over the pork. Serve in a corn tortilla with the pineapple salsa.

This would also go well with stuffed sweet potatoes (see page 100) and a green salad. The marinade also goes well with beef or chicken.

LEON LAMB KOFTE

Another staple on the LEON menu, we serve them either in a wrap, on a superfood salad base, or with chili sauce on brown rice as meatballs. It's totally up to you. The word kofte means "to beat," so let it all out when you mix. The meat should be really bashed around and tenderized.

PREP TIME: 15 MINS · COOK TIME: 10 MINS

1 lb 2 oz **ground lamb**

large handfuls of chopped **fresh oregano** and **thyme**

½ teaspoon each of **ground cumin, coriander, cloves**, and **cardamom**

1 teaspoon **yellow mustard seeds**

1 teaspoon **red chile flakes**

3 cloves of **garlic**, crushed

salt and **freshly ground black pepper**

1 tablespoon **olive oil**

1. Heat the oven to 400°F.

2. Mix all the ingredients except for the oil together. Bash it all together with your hands to combine thoroughly. Roll into egg-size balls.

3. Heat the oil in a skillet over medium heat. Brown the kofte in the oil and make sure to get the outside caramelized. After 4 to 5 minutes, transfer them to a sturdy baking pan and place in the oven for 7 to 10 minutes, until cooked through. Drain on paper towels before serving.

Serve with some salad greens, semidried and baby plum tomatoes, good-quality hummus, sauerkraut, pomegranate seeds, and chili sauce.

ROAST CHICKEN WITH JERUSALEM ARTICHOKES & COPPA DI PARMA

An impressive one-pot roast. Knobbly, nutty Jerusalem artichokes have nothing to do with Jerusalem, or with artichokes. Make the most of them when they're in season. They are brilliant.

PREP TIME: 15 MINS · COOK TIME: 40 MINS

1¼ lb **Jerusalem artichokes**, peeled

4 **leeks**, sliced

20 **fresh sage leaves**, shredded

3½ oz **coppa di Parma slices**

2 cups **strong chicken stock**

1 clove of **garlic**, crushed

6 to 8 **chicken thighs**, skin on and bone in

salt and **freshly ground black pepper**

1. Heat the oven to 350°F.

2. Slice the artichokes into disks about ½ inch thick. Place them into the bottom of a baking dish, followed by a layer of leeks, then the sage, and finally the coppa di Parma, seasoning each layer as you go along.

3. Mix the stock with the garlic and pour the mixture evenly over the ingredients in the baking dish.

4. Set a wire rack over the baking dish. Season the chicken pieces and place them on the rack, skin-side up, so that any juices they give off while cooking drip onto the vegetables below.

5. Place in the oven and roast for about 40 minutes, or until the chicken is cooked through and the artichokes are tender. Leave to cool slightly before serving.

ASIAN FISH BROTH

This broth will banish any colds or flus that may be brewing in your home. Use the spice paste with chicken for a chicken broth, too.

PREP TIME: 15 MINS · COOK TIME: 15 MINS

1¼ cups **coconut water**

1¾ cups **fish stock**

2 stalks of **lemon grass**, chopped

2 **shallots**, sliced

14 oz **firm white fish fillets**, skin removed

2 cups **beansprouts**

3½ oz **sugar snap peas**, sliced

juice of 2 **limes**

1 **red chile**, sliced

leaves from a small bunch of **Thai basil**

salt and **freshly ground black pepper**

FOR THE PASTE

1 × ¾-inch piece of **ginger**, grated

2 cloves of **garlic**, crushed

2 **red chiles**, finely chopped

1 teaspoon **ground turmeric**

2 tablespoons chopped **fresh cilantro stalks**

1 bunch of **scallions**, chopped

1 oz **creamed coconut**, grated

½ teaspoon **salt**

1. Blend together the paste ingredients in a food processor until smooth.

2. Heat the coconut water with the fish stock, lemon grass, and shallots. Whisk in the paste and simmer for about 10 minutes.

3. Add the fish to the broth and cook over low heat for about 5 minutes, until the fish is just cooked. The cooking time will be dependent on the thickness of the fillets.

4. Place the beansprouts and sugar snap peas in a large serving bowl. Add lime juice to the soup broth to taste, check the seasoning, and then ladle the soup over the beansprouts. Scatter with the chile and basil leaves to serve.

You can buy Thai basil frozen from Asian supermarkets. If you can't find it, don't worry. You can use cilantro instead. Do not use regular basil, however, because it's not a good substitute.

DEVILED CALVES' LIVER WITH KALE & PANCETTA

Liver and bacon are a heavenly deviled pair.
We could make more jokes, but you'd think they were offal.

PREP TIME: 20 MINS · COOK TIME: 45 MINS

¼ cup **olive oil**, divided

4 **red onions**, sliced

7 oz **kale**

3½ oz **pancetta lardons**

1 **clove** of garlic, crushed

1 × 14 oz can of **cranberry beans**,
   drained and rinsed

14 oz **calves' liver** slices, trimmed

1 tablespoon **balsamic vinegar**

2 tablespoons snipped **fresh
   chives**

salt and **freshly ground black
   pepper**

FOR THE DEVILED SAUCE

1 **shallot**

1 tablespoon **olive oil**

1 clove of **garlic**, crushed

3 tablespoons **white wine**

½ cup **chicken stock**

2 teaspoons **English mustard**

2 teaspoons **Dijon mustard**

2 teaspoons **tomato paste**

a dash of **Worcestershire sauce**

a dash of **Tabasco**

1 teaspoon **maple syrup**

1. Heat 2 tablespoons of oil in a large pan. Add the sliced onions and cook over low heat for at least 30 minutes. The longer you can cook them for, the sweeter they will be. Season well.

2. While the onions are cooking, make the deviled sauce. Cook the shallot in the olive oil for 5 minutes. Add the garlic and wine, turn up the heat, and reduce to a syrup. Add the stock with the rest of the ingredients, beat together, and simmer for 5 minutes.

3. Remove the central rib from the kale and discard. Blanch the leaves in plenty of boiling salted water for 2 minutes. Drain, refresh in cold water, and squeeze out any excess liquid. Coarsely chop the kale.

4. Heat 1 tablespoon of oil in a pan and cook the pancetta lardons until lightly browned. Add the garlic, cook for a minute, then stir in the kale. Braise for a few minutes, then stir in the cranberry beans. Cook for a few minutes to heat through and season well.

5. Heat the last tablespoon of oil in a large nonstick pan and cook the calves' liver for a minute on either side. The liver should be slightly pink in the middle. The cooking time will depend on the thickness of the slices. Add a splash of balsamic vinegar and season. Remove the liver from the pan and add the deviled sauce to heat through.

6. To serve, spoon the kale and beans onto plates with the liver. Top with the onions and deviled sauce, and scatter with snipped chives to serve.

CELERY ROOT PASTA

Celery root can be cut into tagliatelle-like pasta strips. You can try spiralizing it but it's quite a workout. The best thing to do is use a mandoline slicer to cut it into large disks, then slice these with a knife. We cannot emphasize enough how brilliant a replacement for pasta this is. It doesn't taste remotely like celery root once cooked and coated in these sauces. Serve it to a gluten-eater and they'd be none the wiser. Promise.

PREP TIME: 10 MINS · COOK TIME: 3 MINS

1 large **celery root**, peeled

1 tablespoon **olive oil**

salt and **freshly ground black pepper**

1. Cut the celery root into very thin slices, using a mandoline slicer if you have one. Cut each slice into strips about ¾ inch wide, or into coarse triangles.

2. Cook in a large pan of boiling water for 3 minutes, then drain well and toss with the olive oil. Season very well.

3. Toss with one of the following pasta sauces to serve.

1. CAPER, HERB & EGG DRESSING

PREP TIME: 15 MINS

2 tablespoons **salted capers**, soaked in **cold water**

2 tablespoons **gherkins**, chopped

2 tablespoons **fresh tarragon**, chopped

2 tablespoons **fresh chives**, snipped

2 **shallots**, finely chopped

2 tablespoons **fresh parsley**, chopped

1 tablespoon **Dijon mustard**

1 tablespoon **grain mustard**

2 **egg yolks**

salt and **freshly ground black pepper**

1. Drain the capers and coarsely chop. Mix with the rest of the ingredients. Season well.

2. When the celery root is drained but while it's still hot, toss with the dressing off the heat.

2. SAUSAGE & TOMATO SAUCE

PREP TIME: 10 MINS · COOK TIME: 50 MINS

1 tablespoon **olive oil**

14 oz good-quality **gluten-free pork sausages**

2 teaspoons **ground fennel seeds**

a good pinch of **dried chile flakes**

leaves from 1 sprig of **fresh rosemary**, chopped

5 cloves of **garlic**, finely sliced

3¼ cups canned **diced tomatoes**

salt and **freshly ground black pepper**

1. Heat the oil in a large, deep skillet. Remove the sausage casing and crumble the meat into the pan. Let brown for a few minutes, then push to one side. Add the fennel, chile flakes, rosemary, and garlic. Stir and cook for a minute, then add the tomatoes and stir everything together thoroughly.

2. Bring to a simmer and let cook over low heat for about 45 minutes. Season well and toss with the celery root.

3. LAMB & PEA SAUCE

PREP TIME: 10 MINS · COOK TIME: 1 HOUR 30 MINS

9 oz **lamb shoulder**, cut into
½-inch cubes

1 tablespoon **olive oil**

1 **onion**, finely chopped

2 cloves of **garlic**, crushed

1 cup **chicken** or **lamb stock**

1 tablespoon **red wine vinegar**

1 cup **peas**

a bunch of **fresh parsley**,
shredded

salt and **freshly ground black
pepper**

1. Fry the lamb in the oil until lightly browned. Add the onion and cook over very low heat for about 20 minutes. If the lamb is very fatty, pour away the excess fat.

2. Add the garlic and cook for a minute, then add the stock and vinegar. Season well, cover, and cook for about an hour, or until the lamb is tender.

3. Uncover the pan and reduce the sauce until thick. Add the peas and cook for a minute. Stir in the parsley and season to serve.

1.

3.

2.

✓
P
V
Ve
SF

SWEET POTATO & OKRA STEW

🍴④

A twist on the traditional West African peanut stew. We use peanut butter, and it's magnificent. If okra isn't usually a staple vegetable in your house, buy some and freeze it. It holds its shape well, and won't disintegrate.

PREP TIME: 15 MINS · COOK TIME: 35 MINS

1 tablespoon **coconut oil**

2 **onions**, finely chopped

2 cloves of **garlic**, crushed

1 × ¾-inch piece of **ginger**, grated

1 **red chile**, chopped

2 **sweet potatoes**, peeled and cut into ¾-inch chunks

15 **okra**, sliced

1 teaspoon **ground cumin**

½ teaspoon **ground turmeric**

½ teaspoon **ground cinnamon**

1 teaspoon **smoked paprika**

3 large **tomatoes**, skinned and diced

1½ cups **vegetable stock**

3½ oz **chard**, **kale**, or **collard greens**, shredded

3 tablespoons **smooth peanut butter**

2 tablespoons crushed **unsalted peanuts**

2 tablespoons chopped **fresh cilantro**

salt and **freshly ground black pepper**

1. Heat the oil in a large pan, add the onions, and cook for 10 minutes. Stir in the garlic, ginger, chile, sweet potatoes, and sliced okra. Stir well and cook for 2 minutes, sprinkling the vegetables with the spices.

2. Add the diced tomatoes and season well. Pour in the stock and bring to a simmer. Cook over low heat for about 15 minutes, or until the sweet potato is tender.

3. Add the greens and cover the pan. Simmer for 2 minutes, or until the greens are tender. Stir in the peanut butter. Add a little extra stock if it seems too thick. Cook for another 5 minutes, and then check the seasoning.

4. Serve sprinkled with crushed peanuts and chopped cilantro.

This would be a good accompaniment to our Ehtiopian flatbread (see page 250).

PIZZA

Jo, who designed this book, is obsessed with pizza. She's got a pizza phone cover and pizza socks. She's now obsessed with this. We topped half with pissaladière and half with tomato sauce, griddled zucchini and chile for a bit of variety. The paleo cauliflower base will steal a pizza your heart.

PREP TIME: 10 MINS · COOK TIME: 25 MINS

1 small **cauliflower**

1 tablespoon **olive oil**

1 cup **almond flour** (or **ground almonds**)

2 **eggs**

1 teaspoon **nutritional yeast** (or similar, optional)

salt and **freshly ground black pepper**

1. Heat the oven to 400°F.

2. To make the pizza crust, remove the florets from the cauliflower and blitz in a food processor until they resemble couscous. Heat the oil in a large skillet and fry the cauliflower for about 5 minutes, stirring well.

3. Let the cauliflower cool, then place in a food processor with the other ingredients and season well. Blitz to combine, then turn out onto a baking pan lined with nonstick parchment paper. With a spatula or your fingers, spread the mixture out to make a circle (about 12 inches wide) or a rectangle. Aim to make it about ¼ inch thick.

4. Bake in the oven for about 20 minutes, or until it starts to turn golden brown. Remove from the oven and set aside while you make the topping.

PISSALADIÈRE

PREP TIME: 10 MINS · COOK TIME: 55 MINS

3 tablespoons **olive oil**

3 **onions**, thinly sliced

3 **red onions**, thinly sliced

a sprig of **fresh thyme**

1 **bay leaf**

1 clove of **garlic**, crushed

10 **anchovies** in oil, divided

8 **baby plum tomatoes**, sliced

15 **black olives**, stoned

salt

1. Heat the oil in a large shallow pan. Add all the onions, sprinkle with a little salt, add the thyme and bay leaf, and cook gently over low heat for about 40 minutes without browning.

2. Add the garlic and 3 of the anchovies and cook for a few minutes, or until the anchovies have melted into the onions.

3. Spread the onions over the pizza crust and arrange the remaining anchovies, sliced tomatoes, and black olives on top.

4. Put the pissaladière back into the oven for 10 minutes to finish cooking.

OTHER SERVING IDEAS

tomato sauce (see page 88) with grilled **eggplant**, **olives**, and **oregano**

slow-cooked leeks, **prosciutto**, and **sage**

zucchini, **peppers**, **mint**, and **capers**

SPRING CHICKEN

This chicken with spring vegetables, dumplings, and tarragon gremolata is not no spring chicken.

PREP TIME: 15 MINS · COOK TIME: 30 MINS

4 **chicken breasts**

1 tablespoon **olive oil**

2 cups **chicken stock**

8 small **carrots**, peeled

8 **baby turnips**, peeled

8 **baby leeks** or **scallions**, trimmed

3½ oz **fava beans**

3½ oz **asparagus**, cut into ¾-inch
    pieces

¾ cup **peas**

salt and **freshly ground black
    pepper**

FOR THE DUMPLINGS

3 tablespoons **arrowroot**

¾ cup toasted **ground almonds**

a pinch of **baking soda**

½ teaspoon **salt**

about ¼ cup **chicken stock**, plus
    extra for poaching

FOR THE GREMOLATA

1 tablespoon chopped **fresh
    parsley**

1 tablespoon chopped **fresh
    tarragon**

very fine zest of 2 **lemons**

2 cloves of **garlic**, minced

1. Season the chicken breasts with salt and pepper. Heat the oil in a large pan and add the chicken skin-side down. Cook for a few minutes, or until the skin is lightly browned. Turn over and seal the other side for 2 minutes.

2. Pour in the stock and bring to a simmer. Add the carrots and turnips and cook gently for 5 minutes with the chicken. Add the rest of the vegetables and cook for 5 minutes. Turn off the heat and let rest. Check the chicken is firm to the touch and cooked through.

3. Mix together the arrowroot, almonds, baking soda, and salt in a bowl. Slowly add the stock until you have a wet but manageable dough (it will be on the wet side of manageable). Let the mixture stand for 15 minutes to thicken. Roll into small balls about ¾ inch in diameter if you can, but you may find it easier to use two spoons to make quenelles (think of a fancy ice-cream scoop).

4. Heat the extra chicken stock in a small pan to the depth of ¾ inch. When it's simmering, add the dumplings and poach for 10 minutes over low heat. Add to the chicken.

5. Mix together the parsley, tarragon, lemon zest, and garlic and scatter the chicken and vegetables with the mixture just before serving.

You could easily
make this a chicken
dish with seasonal
vegetables in late
summer or fall.

FEIJOADA SOUP

Feijoada is a Brazilian stew made with different cuts of pork: smoked, fatty, and extremities. You can use a pressure cooker to speed up the cooking of the meat. Precooking a smoked ham hock results in really good stock that you can use in the soup.

PREP TIME: 20 MINS · COOK TIME: I HOUR 20 MINS

1 tablespoon **olive oil**

2½ oz **pancetta lardons**

7 oz **cooking chorizo**, cut into chunks

10½ oz **pork shoulder**, cut into ¾-inch dice

10½ oz **pork ribs**

1 **red chile**, chopped

3 **onions**, chopped

1 **red bell pepper**, chopped

4 cloves of **garlic**, crushed

2 **bay leaves**

a pinch of **dried thyme**

2 teaspoons **smoked paprika**

2 strips of **orange zest**

1 quart **chicken or ham stock**, plus extra for thinning

1 × 14 oz can of **black beans**

1 cup **edamame beans**

3½ oz flaked **ham hock** (optional)

3½ oz **kale**

2 teaspoons **red wine vinegar**

salt and **freshly ground black pepper**

FOR THE FAROFA

3 tablespoons **olive oil**

1 **onion**, finely chopped

1¾ cups **cassava flour**

a pinch of **salt**

1. Heat the oil in a large pan and add the lardons and chorizo. Cook over medium heat for 5 minutes until lightly browned. Remove with a slotted spoon and set aside.

2. Turn the heat up and add the pork shoulder and ribs. Brown the meat for a few minutes and season well. Remove from the pan and set aside with the lardons.

3. Add the chile, onions, red bell pepper, and garlic to the pan. Cook over low heat for 5 minutes, then add the bay leaves, thyme, paprika, and orange zest. Return all the meat to the pan and cook together for 5 minutes, then add the stock.

4. Bring to a boil and simmer for about an hour, or until you can flake the pork off of the bone. Add the black beans, edamame, ham hock, and kale. Bring back to a simmer and let cook for a few minutes until the kale has wilted. Season and add a little vinegar. Add extra stock to thin the soup to the required consistency.

5. To make the farofa, heat the oil in a large, heavy skillet. Cook the onion for 5 minutes, then add the flour and season with the salt. Turn the heat down and cook the flour for about 10 minutes, stirring constantly, so the flour becomes slightly toasted and crunchy.

6. Serve the soup with a sprinkling of farofa and the tomatillo salsa from page 248, if liked.

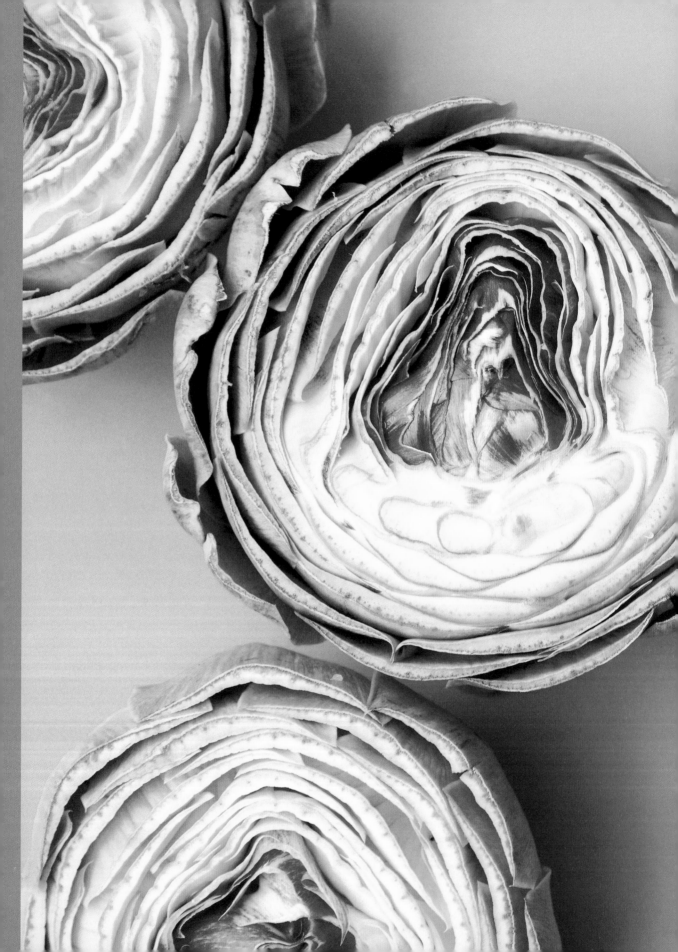

MEALS FOR A CROWD

QUICK
MIDWINTER BRISKET

In the bleak midwinter, this brisket and root vegetable medley will brighten up suppertime. If you want to save energy, money, and time (we do), you can make this in a pressure cooker. If you're using a Dutch oven, however, double the cooking times.

PREP TIME: 20 MINS · COOK TIME: 1 HOUR 20 MINS

about 2¼ to 4½ lb **beef brisket**

1 teaspoon **salt**

1 teaspoon **freshly ground black pepper**

1 tablespoon **olive oil**

4 large **onions**, thinly sliced

1 **bay leaf**

1 sprig of **fresh thyme**

6 cloves of **garlic**, crushed

1 tablespoon **tomato paste**

½ cup **red wine**

a dash of **balsamic vinegar**

2 cups **beef or chicken stock**

1 tablespoon **Dijon mustard**

1 tablespoon **wholegrain mustard**

10½ oz **small carrots**, peeled

10½ oz **turnips**, peeled and quartered

10½ oz **rutabaga**, peeled and cut into large chunks

10 **dumplings** (see page 164)

1. Trim most of the fat and connective tissue off of the brisket, leaving a thin layer of fat. Rub with salt and pepper. Heat the oil in a pressure cooker until quite hot, and brown the outside of the brisket. If the meat is too large to fit in the pan in one piece, cut it in half or thirds.

2. Remove the meat from the pan, turn the heat down to medium, and add the onions along with the bay leaf and thyme. Cook for 5 minutes, then add the garlic. Stir for a minute, then add the tomato paste, wine, vinegar, and stock. Bring to a simmer and return the meat to the pan. Attach the lid to the pressure cooker and cook on high pressure for about an hour.

3. Allow the cooker to cool down for 10 minutes before opening. Remove the meat from the pan and cut into thick slices across the grain. Whisk the mustards into the sauce, then return the sliced meat to the pan along with the vegetables.

4. Place the lid back on the pan and cook on low pressure for another 30 minutes. In the last 20 minutes of cooking, separately poach the dumplings (see page 164 for method). When cool enough, transfer the meat, dumplings, and vegetables from the pan to a platter and keep warm. Turn up the heat and reduce the sauce to a coating consistency. Pour the sauce over the meat before serving and add the dumplings, but handle these gently because they're delicate!

This is great served with braised Savoy cabbage. Feel free to use any type of root vegetables you can get your hands on.

SMOKED DUCK, FIG & WALNUT SALAD

Fall is the fig's time to shine. They pair so well with the gamey and rich smoked duck.

PREP TIME: 15 MINS

FOR THE DRESSING

2 tablespoons **walnut oil**

1 tablespoon **mild olive oil**

1 tablespoon **balsamic vinegar**

juice of 1 **clementine**

1 teaspoon **Dijon mustard**

1 teaspoon **raw honey**

a pinch of **cayenne pepper**

salt and **freshly ground black pepper**

FOR THE SALAD

1 head of **red Belgian endive**

1½ cups **frisée**

leaves from ¼ **head of radicchio**

a small bunch of **watercress**

½ cup **walnuts**, toasted and coarsely chopped

4 **figs**, quartered

seeds from ½ **pomegranate**

1 **blood orange** (or **clementine**), skinned and sliced

2 **smoked duck breasts**, thinly sliced

1. Whisk all the dressing ingredients together to emulsify and season well.

2. Separate the leaves from the Belgian endive and place in a bowl with the rest of the salad leaves.

3. Toss the leaves with most of the salad dressing and place on a platter, reserving about one-quarter of the dressing. Top with the rest of the salad ingredients and drizzle with the rest of the dressing to serve.

If you can't find smoked duck, you could use the confit duck recipe on page 192, or just a regular cooked duck breast.

PROSCIUTTO, PORCINI & LEEK "LASAGNE"

Using celery root where once was pasta adds a creamy, earthy layer to this twist on an Italian classic, *vincisgrassi*. At first blush, this recipe seems really complicated but it's actually very simple. All the preparation can be done ahead of time, and the lasagne can be assembled and cooked just before serving.

PREP TIME: 40 MINS · COOK TIME: 1 HOUR 10 MINS

½ oz **dried porcini mushrooms**

1 cup **boiling water**

1 **celery root**, peeled

¼ cup **olive oil**, divided

4 to 6 **leeks**, trimmed and halved

7 oz **spinach**

10½ oz **cauliflower florets**

1 cup **almond milk**

a pinch of **ground nutmeg**

1 **shallot**, finely chopped

1 clove of **garlic**, crushed

1 tablespoon **truffle oil**

2 tablespoons chopped **fresh parsley**

2 teaspoons chopped **fresh tarragon**

3½ oz **prosciutto slices**

extra **truffle oil** for drizzling (optional)

salt and **freshly ground black pepper**

To peel a celery root it's best to use a serrated knife and saw around it. A vegetable peeler won't really work.

1. Heat the oven to 400°F.

2. Soak the dried porcini in the boiling water.

3. Thinly slice the celery root to about the thickness of a lasagne sheet, then toss the sheets in 2 tablespoons of olive oil and season. Lay the celery root on baking pans and cook in the oven for about 20 minutes, until just soft. (It doesn't matter if the sheets are overlapping.) Remove from the oven and set aside.

4. Cook the leeks for a few minutes in boiling salted water until tender. Remove from the pan, drain well, and season.

5. Heat 1 tablespoon of olive oil in a large pan, add the spinach, season, and cook until wilted. Tip into a colander to drain. When cool enough, squeeze out any excess moisture and chop coarsely.

6. Steam the cauliflower florets until tender. Using a hand-held stick blender, blend with the almond milk until very smooth and season well with nutmeg, salt, and pepper to make the equivalent of a béchamel sauce.

7. Drain the soaked porcini, reserving the soaking liquid. Chop the mushrooms finely and cook in the remaining tablespoon of olive oil with the chopped shallots for 5 minutes. Add the garlic and cook for a further minute, then tip in the soaking liquid. Bring to a boil and reduce the liquid until it has a thick coating consistency. Stir in the cauliflower purée, truffle oil, and herbs. Season well.

8. To assemble the lasagne, layer up the ingredients in a baking dish. First add a little of the sauce to the bottom of the dish and spread it out with the back of a spoon. Top with the pieces of celery root and the slices of prosciutto. Add a single layer of leeks, cutting them to fit the dish, and scatter with some chopped spinach. Drizzle with a little more sauce and repeat the process until all the ingredients have been used up, finishing with a layer of celery root topped with the porcini sauce.

9. Bake in the oven for about 25 minutes, then remove and let stand for 10 minutes before serving. The dish can be drizzled with extra truffle oil to serve, if you like.

MEATLOAF

We would do anything for loaf, but we won't do that.

PREP TIME: 20 MINS · COOK TIME: 1 HOUR 10 MINS

1 oz **dried porcini mushrooms**

1 cup **boiling water**

2 tablespoons **olive oil**

1 **onion**, finely chopped

2 stalks of **celery**, finely chopped

1 **carrot**, finely chopped

1 **leek**, finely chopped

1 **red bell pepper**, finely chopped

6 **scallions**, chopped

2 cloves of **garlic**, crushed

1 lb 2 oz **ground veal**

1 lb 2 oz **ground pork**

5½ oz **chicken livers**, trimmed

2 teaspoons **chili sauce**

2 teaspoons **tomato paste**

½ cup **almond milk**

3 **eggs**, beaten

¾ cup **ground almonds** (or
  gluten-free bread crumbs)

½ teaspoon **ground cumin**

½ teaspoon **ground nutmeg**

½ teaspoon **paprika**

2 teaspoons **freshly ground black
  pepper**

salt

FOR THE SCOTCH EGGS

10 **eggs**

¾ cup **rice flour**

1½ cups **gluten-free bread crumbs**
  or **polenta**

canola oil, for deep-frying

1. Heat the oven to 325°F.

2. Soak the dried porcini in the boiling water. Set aside for 15 minutes.

3. Heat the oil in a large pan and cook all the finely chopped vegetables (use a food processor to get them super fine) for about 15 minutes over low heat, making sure they do not brown or stick to the bottom of the pan.

4. Drain the porcini, reserving the liquid, and chop the mushrooms finely. Add to the pan of vegetables with the garlic and cook for another 5 minutes. Add the contents of the pan to a bowl and let cool. The porcini soaking liquor can be frozen and used in risottos or gravy.

5. Add the veal and pork to the vegetable mixture. Blitz the chicken livers in a food processor for a few seconds and pour into the bowl. Add the rest of the ingredients and mix well so that everything is evenly distributed.

6. It's a good idea to fry and taste a little of the mixture, so that the seasoning can be adjusted before cooking. Once you're satisfied, spoon the mixture into a lined loaf pan and place in a bain-marie in the oven for an hour.

7. To serve, turn out onto a serving dish and slice.

  ## SCOTCH EGGS

The uncooked meatloaf mixture makes the perfect casing for Scotch eggs. Scotch eggs are great. This recipe is great. It is a rather wet mixture, but this helps to maintain the moisture through cooking.

PREP TIME: 15 MINS · COOK TIME: 16 MINS

1. Boil 8 of the eggs for 5 minutes, then refresh in cold water and peel. Meanwhile, beat the remaining eggs together well.

2. Wrap the boiled eggs in a ¾-inch layer of the meatloaf mixture.

3. Roll the eggs first in rice flour, then in beaten egg, and finally either gluten-free bread crumbs or polenta.

4. Heat the oil for deep-frying to 350°F and fry the Scotch eggs for 10 minutes, until golden brown. Drain on paper towels before serving.

CHICKPEA TAGLIATELLE

This chickpea pasta is just the ticket for all the chic chicks in your life.
Jane made this for a gluten-free pasta night in her kitchen, and all the children loved it.

**PREP TIME: 30 MINS · SOAK TIME: OVERNIGHT · CHILL TIME: OVERNIGHT
COOK TIME: 1 HOUR 10 MINS**

1 cup **chickpeas**, soaked overnight

6 cloves of **garlic**, crushed

½ **leek**, finely sliced

½ **red onion**, diced

2 **cherry tomatoes**, halved

1 small **dried chile**, finely sliced

1 sprig of **fresh rosemary**

¾ cup **olive oil**, for frying

salt and **freshly ground black pepper**

FOR THE PASTA DOUGH

3 cups **gram flour**

3 tablespoons **arrowroot**

a pinch of **salt**

3 **eggs**

millet flour, for rolling

1. Place the gram flour, arrowroot, and salt in a food processor. Blitz, adding the eggs one by one. Empty the dough onto a clean surface and knead lightly to bring it together. If the dough feels sticky, add extra gram flour. Divide the dough into 4 and seal in plastic wrap. Let chill in the fridge for about 30 minutes.

2. Roll out each piece of dough on a surface sprinkled with a little millet flour. The dough can now be fed through a pasta machine until fairly thin. Alternatively it can be rolled out by hand with a rolling pin. Cut the pasta sheets into strips about ½ inch wide then transfer to a lightly floured tray.

3. Drain the chickpeas and put them into a pan. Cover with water and add the vegetables, chile, and rosemary. Bring to a boil, then simmer for about an hour, until the chickpeas are tender. Make sure the chickpeas are always covered with water.

4. Remove the vegetables along with ½ cup of liquid and blitz together to make your sauce. Return it to the pan and stir it into the chickpeas. Season well.

5. Divide the tagliatelle coarsely into thirds. Cook two-thirds in lots of boiling salted water. Fry the final third in hot olive oil until the pieces of pasta crisp up. Remove with a slotted spoon and let drain on a plate lined with paper towels.

6. Combine the cooked pasta with the chickpeas, adding a little extra water so the pasta isn't dry. Season well and add the fried crisp pasta pieces before serving.

PIGEON & SQUASH SALAD

Pigeons are gamey-tasting birds, with a deep nutty flavor. Remember, you want a wood pigeon, not an urban pigeon. If you can't source it, partridge, guinea fowl, or pheasant would also be delicious. This is a meal fit for a proper fall afternoon.

PREP TIME: 20 MINS · COOK TIME: 50 MINS

10½ oz **beets**

5 tablespoons **olive oil**, divided

10½ oz **butternut squash**, peeled and cut into ½-inch slices

8 **pigeon breasts**

8 slices of **prosciutto**

1 tablespoon **walnut oil**

1 tablespoon **pumpkin seed oil**

1 tablespoon **sherry vinegar**

3½ oz **mixed baby leaves**

½ cup **toasted walnuts**

2 tablespoons **toasted pumpkin seeds**

salt and **freshly ground black pepper**

1. Heat the oven to 350°F.

2. Peel the beets and cut into fine dice. Toss with 2 tablespoons of olive oil to coat and season. Place on a baking pan and cover with foil. Bake for about 40 minutes or until tender.

3. After the diced beets have been in the oven for 10 minutes, toss the squash in 1 tablespoon of olive oil and season well. Place on a baking pan and roast for about 30 minutes, or until tender. Allow both vegetables to cool. This way, both your vegetables will be out of the oven at the same time.

4. Season the pigeon breasts and heat 1 tablespoon of the oil in a large nonstick skillet. Cook the pigeon for about 2 minutes on each side, then let rest. Fry the prosciutto slices for a minute to crisp up, and set aside with the pigeon.

5. Whisk the walnut oil, pumpkin seed oil, and the remaining tablespoon of olive oil with the sherry vinegar to emulsify and season well. Toss the leaves in half the dressing and arrange on a plate with the diced beets and squash.

6. Slice the pigeon and arrange on top of the salad with the prosciutto. Scatter with the seeds and nuts and drizzle with the rest of the dressing to serve.

BEEF SHIN & VEGETABLE SOUP

The initial cooking of the beef can be done in a pressure cooker to save time. The vegetables given are only a suggestion—this is a good soup for using up all those leftover greens and roots that accumulate at the bottom of your crisper and leave you a little stumped.

PREP TIME: 20 MINS · COOK TIME: 2 HOURS 10 MINS

1 tablespoon **rice bran oil**

1¾ lb **beef shin on the bone**, cut into 4 pieces

2 **onions**, sliced

1 × 1¼-inch cube of **ginger**, sliced

6 cloves of **garlic**, sliced

2 **red chiles**, sliced

2 **star anise**

1 tablespoon **tamari**

1 quart **beef** or **chicken stock**

3½ oz **rice noodles** (or **soba noodles**)

3½ oz **purple sprouting broccoli**, trimmed

3½ oz **carrots** and/or **turnips**, cut into thin batons

¾ cup sliced **mushrooms**

3½ oz **bok choy** or **other greens**

1 tablespoon chopped **fresh cilantro**

1 tablespoon snipped **fresh chives**

1. Heat the oil in a large pan and brown the pieces of beef. Remove from the pan, then turn down the heat and add the onions, ginger, garlic, and chiles. Cook for a minute, then add the star anise, tamari, and stock. Bring to a simmer and return the beef to the pan. Cover and cook over low heat for 2 hours, or until the beef is tender.

2. In a separate pan, cover the noodles with boiling water and let stand for 10 minutes. Drain well.

3. Add the vegetables to the soup, adding extra stock if required. Cook for another 5 minutes. Take the soup pan off of the heat, add the rice noodles, and scatter with the herbs to serve.

STUFFED SQUID

These squid are full of a fennel and chard stuffing, and will even convert fennel haters. Don't overfill them with the stuffing, because the squid will shrink once it's cooked.

PREP TIME: 30 MINS · COOK TIME: 30 MINS

32 **small squid**, cleaned

¼ cup **olive oil**

4 cloves of **garlic**, crushed

1 lb 2 oz good **tomatoes**, skinned and chopped

2 bunches of **fresh basil**, shredded

extra virgin olive oil, for drizzling

FOR THE STUFFING

2 tablespoons **olive oil**

2 **shallots**, minced

1 head of **fennel**, finely chopped

2 teaspoons **ground fennel seeds**

1 teaspoon **chile flakes**

2 cloves of **garlic**, chopped

4 **anchovies**, chopped

3½ oz **rainbow chard**, cooked

1 cup **ground almonds**

salt and **freshly ground black pepper**

1. Heat the olive oil for the stuffing in a large pan. Add the shallot and fennel and cook for 10 minutes, or until tender. Stir in the ground fennel seeds, chile flakes, and garlic and cook for a minute. Tip in the anchovies, then remove from the heat and stir until the anchovies dissolve.

2. Squeeze any excess moisture out of the chard and chop finely. Add to the pan and cook for a minute. Season well. Remove from the heat and stir in the almonds. Let cool.

3. Stuff each squid with the fennel and chard stuffing. Tuck the tentacles back into the opening of each squid tube and secure with a toothpick.

4. Heat the olive oil in a large nonstick skillet. Add all the squid and brown over high heat for 2 minutes. Remove from the pan with a slotted spoon.

5. Add the garlic to the pan and stir for a minute. Tip in the tomatoes and cook for 5 minutes over medium heat. Stir in the basil and return the squid to the pan. Cook over low heat for 10 minutes. Season well and drizzle with good extra virgin olive oil to serve.

These are brilliant served with a large glass of white wine (or, as Jane calls it, lady fuel).

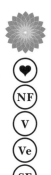

POTATO GNOCCHI

Knock, knock, gnocchi on heaven's door. You need floury russet potatoes for this recipe.

PREP TIME: 10 MINS · COOK TIME: 50 MINS

1 lb 2 oz **russet potatoes**
¼ cup **potato starch**
¼ cup **arrowroot**
2 teaspoons **cornstarch**
salt

1. Heat the oven to 350°F.

2. Place the potatoes directly on the shelf of the oven and bake for about 45 minutes, or until cooked through. The time will depend on the size of the potatoes. When you take them out of the oven, cut each potato in half to release steam and let the moisture evaporate.

3. Sift together all the dry ingredients and mix well. Sprinkle about one-quarter of the flour mixture onto a clean dry work surface. (You will probably not need to use all of this mixture. The amount required will really depend on the starch content of your potatoes.)

4. Bring lots of salted water to a boil.

5. While the potatoes are still hot, scoop out the flesh into a potato ricer and rice the potatoes directly onto the floured surface. Sprinkle with more flour mixture (but keep a little in reserve).

6. Bring the dough together with your hands and knead briefly. It should be soft, but manageable. Pinch off a small piece of the dough and drop it into the boiling water as a tester. If it falls apart add more flour mixture to the dough. If not, you're good to go. Roll the dough into long logs and cut into pieces about ½-inch wide. Press the top of each piece with the prongs of a fork and dust with the remaining flour mixture. This adds texture and helps the gnocchi take on the flavor of whatever sauce you use with it.

7. Simmer for a few minutes until all the gnocchi have come to the surface. Transfer to a plate using a slotted spoon. The gnocchi can be used immediately, with a sauce, or refrigerated and fried in olive oil later.

We served this with 1 tablespoon of truffle paste mixed with a few tablespoons of cashew cream (see page 270, but omit the vanilla and honey) and a little of the pasta water.

TORTILLA SOUP

Poaching a chicken in stock will give you enough meat for the soup and loads of well flavored stock for the base.

PREP TIME: 15 MINS · COOK TIME: 1 HOUR

6 **corn tortillas**

¼ cup **olive oil**, divided

6 **red chiles**, divided

1 quart **chicken broth**

kernels from 2 **cobs of corn**, or

1 × 14 oz can of **kernel corn**, drained

1 **onion**, finely chopped

2 cloves of **garlic**, crushed

1 sprig of **fresh thyme**

1 teaspoon **ground cumin**

1 teaspoon **smoked paprika**

½ teaspoon **ground cinnamon**

1 × 14 oz can of **tomatoes**

1 **cooked chicken** (meat removed from carcass) or 4 cooked **chicken breasts**, shredded

2 teaspoons **raw honey**

10½ oz **rainbow chard**, stems removed and leaves shredded

juice of 1 **lime**

2 **avocados**, chopped

fresh cilantro, chopped

salt and **freshly ground black pepper**

1. Heat the oven to 350°F.

2. Cut the tortillas into strips ½ inch wide. Toss them in half the olive oil and bake in the oven for about 10 minutes, or until golden and crisp. Set aside.

3. Chop 4 of the chiles, removing the seeds, then put them into a pan with the chicken stock. Bring to a boil, then let simmer for 15 minutes. Slice the remaining 2 chiles and set aside.

4. Cook the corn kernels in the remaining oil in a skillet over high heat until they are slightly browned. Add the onions, sliced chiles, garlic, and thyme. Cook for 5 minutes, then add the spices and stir well. Add the tomatoes, including the juice from the can, and bring to a simmer. Cook for about 20 minutes over low heat.

5. Blend the chicken stock with the large chiles, using a hand-held stick blender, and add to the tomato sauce. Return to a simmer and add the shredded chicken, honey, and chard. Cook for another 10 minutes, adding more stock if required.

6. Finish with a good squeeze of lime juice and check the seasoning.

7. To serve, divide half the tortilla pieces between 6 bowls. Ladle the soup over the top and finish with the rest of the tortilla strips, avocado, and fresh cilantro.

MEALS FOR A CROWD

SPICED CHICKEN LIVER SALAD
WITH MUSTARD SEED VINAIGRETTE

A zingy, summer dinner party masterpiece.

PREP TIME: 15 MINS · COOK TIME: 10 MINS

14 oz **chicken livers**

2 tablespoons **garam masala**

2 tablespoons **rice bran oil**

5½ oz **green snap beans**, trimmed

1 cup **frisée**

3½ oz **cherry tomatoes**, halved

1 head of **Belgian endive**

½ cup **cooked Puy lentils**

1 **globe artichoke**, prepared and
cooked or 3½ oz **deli artichokes**

FOR THE DRESSING

1 tablespoon **olive oil**

2 tablespoons **mustard seeds**

1 **shallot**, finely chopped

2 tablespoons **apple cider vinegar**

1 tablespoon **Dijon mustard**

1 teaspoon **maple syrup**

3 tablespoons **canola oil**

salt and **freshly ground black
pepper**

1. To make the dressing heat the olive oil in a small skillet and add the mustard seeds. When the seeds start to pop, cover the pan and take off the heat. Whisk together the rest of the dressing ingredients until emulsified. Season and add the mustard seeds.

2. Trim the chicken livers and toss with the garam masala. Heat the rice bran oil in a large nonstick skillet and fry the chicken livers for 2 to 3 minutes until they are lightly browned and pink in the middle. Set aside.

3. Cook the green beans in lots of boiling salted water for 3 minutes. Drain and refresh in cold water.

4. Toss the beans, frisée, tomatoes, and endive with a little of the dressing. Arrange on a plate and scatter with the cooked lentils and artichoke. Top with the chicken livers and any juices that have gathered in the pan. Drizzle with more dressing to serve.

**If chicken livers
aren't your thing, try this
with mushrooms, or
chicken breast.**

CONFIT DUCK

Confit duck has so many uses, and makes you feel like you've just graduated from Le Cordon Bleu. It keeps for up to two weeks preserved in its fat (which is great for roasting vegetables with), and can be taken out, crisped up quickly, and used in all the variations we've come up with here. If you can't find a jar of duck fat, heat the duck trimmings long and slow in a low oven to render the fat. Or just use oil instead.

PREP TIME: 10 MINS · SALT TIME: OVERNIGHT
COOK TIME: 2 HOURS 15 MINS

6 **duck legs**

¼ cup **rock salt**

1 tablespoon **black peppercorns**, crushed

6 cloves of **garlic**, sliced

5 sprigs of **fresh thyme**

3 **bay leaves**

1½ lb **duck fat**

1. Dry the duck legs. Mix together the salt, pepper, garlic, thyme, and bay leaves. Sprinkle one-third of the mixture onto a platter or dish onto which all the duck legs will fit snugly. Set the duck legs on the salt mixture, skin-side down, and sprinkle with the remaining mixture. Cover, and let stand in the fridge overnight, or for at least 12 hours.

2. Heat the oven to 250°F.

3. Take the duck legs out of the cure and rub off any excess salt. Pat dry with paper towels and place in a deep-sided baking pan, skin-side up. Add some of the sliced garlic, thyme, and bay leaves from the cure. Spoon over the duck fat and cover the baking pan with foil. Cook in a low oven for about 2 hours, or until the meat is tender. Remove from the oven and let cool in the fat.

4. Place the duck legs and fat in the fridge, where they will keep up to 2 weeks.

5. To cook, remove the legs from the fat, scraping off any excess. Heat an ovenproof skillet and put the legs in, skin-side down. Cook for 2 minutes, then flip the chicken over and add to a hot oven for 5 to 10 minutes, until the skin is crisp and brown. Serve with one of the accompaniments overleaf.

1.

2.

3.

1. CASSOULET

PREP TIME: 15 MINS · COOK TIME: 40 MINS

1 tablespoon **duck fat**

7 oz **gluten-free pork sausages**, cut into chunks

1 **onion**, chopped

1 **carrot**, chopped

1 stalk of **celery**, chopped

3 cloves of **garlic**, crushed

2 teaspoons **fennel seeds**, crushed

a pinch of **dried chile flakes**

2 teaspoons chopped **fresh rosemary**

½ × 14 oz can of **diced tomatoes**

1 × 14 oz can of **cannellini beans**, drained and rinsed

¾ cup **chicken stock**

1 tablespoon chopped **fresh parsley**

salt and **freshly ground black pepper**

1. Heat the duck fat in a large skillet. Brown the sausages in the fat and remove from the pan.

2. Add the vegetables and cook over low heat for 15 minutes without browning. Add the garlic, fennel seeds, chile flakes, and rosemary. Cook for a minute, then tip in the diced tomatoes and the sausages.

3. Simmer for 10 minutes, then add the beans and stock. Cook for another 10 minutes, then check the seasoning and serve with the duck, scattered with parsley.

2. MIDDLE EASTERN SLAW

PREP TIME: 10 MINS

1 large **carrot**, grated

1 **red onion**, finely chopped

1 clove of **garlic**, crushed

1 **red chile**, chopped

¼ small **red cabbage**, finely shredded

1 **kohlrabi**, grated

1 tablespoon chopped **fresh parsley**

1 tablespoon chopped **fresh mint**

1 **orange**, skin and pith discarded, chopped

1 teaspoon **pomegranate molasses**

2 tablespoons **pine nuts**, toasted

2 tablespoons **olive oil**

1 tablespoon **balsamic vinegar**

salt and **freshly ground black pepper**

1. Toss all the ingredients together.

2. Season well and serve with duck.

These accompaniments all serve 6 people.

3. DUCK RAGÙ

The duck ragù recipe comes from Ed at the Curator Kitchen in Totnes, in Devon. Ed normally serves it with pappardelle. He cooks the sauce for hours, but we have tried to cut down the cooking time here. We'd recommend this sauce with our celery root or chickpea pastas (see pages 158 and 178).

PREP TIME: 30 MINS · COOK TIME: 1 HOUR 30 MINS

9 oz **gluten-free pasta** of choice

½ **Savoy cabbage**, shredded

1 tablespoon **olive oil**

3 tablespoons chopped **fresh parsley**

salt and **freshly ground black pepper**

FOR THE RAGÙ

2 tablespoons **olive oil**

2 tablespoons **duck fat**

1 **onion**, chopped

2 stalks of **celery**, chopped

1 **leek**, chopped

2 **carrots**, chopped

1 **bay leaf**

2 **cloves**

1 × ¾-inch stick of **cinnamon**

1 **star anise**

2 strips of **orange zest**

4 cloves of **garlic**, crushed

1 × 14 oz can of **diced tomatoes**

4 **cooked duck legs**

1 cup **red wine**

1 cup **chicken** or **duck stock**

salt and **freshly ground black pepper**

1. Heat the oil and duck fat for the ragù in a large pan. Add the chopped vegetables, bay leaf, spices, and orange zest, and cook for about 30 minutes over low heat. Add the garlic and cook for another minute, then tip in the tomatoes and simmer for another 15 minutes.

2. Take the meat off the duck legs and chop into large chunks. Reserve the meat, then add the wine, bones, and stock to the pan. Bring to a boil and simmer until the sauce has thickened. Remove the bones, spices, and orange zest, then take out half the sauce and blend the rest with a hand-held stick blender until smooth. Return the unblended sauce to the pan and mix with the smooth sauce.

3. Add the duck pieces to the sauce and simmer for about another 30 minutes (or longer if you have the time). If it gets too dry at any stage, add more chicken stock or boiling water. Season well.

4. Cook the pasta in lots of boiling water following the package directions. Add the cabbage to the pan 2 minutes before the pasta is ready. Drain well, season, and toss with a little olive oil.

5. Toss the pasta and cabbage with the duck sauce, and serve scattered with lots of chopped parsley.

LEON LAMB & RHUBARB KORESH

A fresh, clean, and complex spring stew. Complex tasting, not making. We've suggested using diced lamb shoulder here, but you could use ground lamb, too.

PREP TIME: 15 MINS · COOK TIME: I HOUR 45 MINS

2 **onions**, peeled and chopped

2 tablespoons **olive oil**, divided

1½ lb **lamb shoulder**, diced

1 teaspoon **ground turmeric**

1¼ cups **chicken stock**

1 bunch of **fresh flat-leaf parsley**, finely chopped

1 bunch of **fresh mint**, finely chopped

1 bunch of **fresh cilantro**, finely chopped

a small pinch of **saffron**, soaked in 2 tablespoons **hot water**

juice of 1 **lime**

1 lb 2 oz **rhubarb**, cut into bite-size pieces

coconut sugar, to taste

extra herbs, chopped, to finish

salt and **freshly ground black pepper**

1. In a Dutch oven, soften the onion in half the olive oil for 5 minutes, then remove from the pot and set aside.

2. Brown the meat in batches in the same pot over high heat. You may need to add a little more oil. When all the meat is browned, return the onions to the pan, and season with salt, pepper, and turmeric. Add the stock, or enough just to cover. Bring to a boil, then turn the heat down to a simmer, cover, and cook for about 1 hour on low heat.

3. Meanwhile, in a skillet, heat the remaining oil and fry the parsley, mint, and cilantro, stirring all the time, for about 7 to 10 minutes. This concentrates their flavors and gives them texture.

4. Add the fried herbs to the lamb, after its hour of cooking, along with the saffron and the lime juice. Bring back to a simmer and cook for 5 to 10 minutes.

5. Now add the rhubarb, and simmer for 10 to 15 minutes.

6. Taste for seasoning. You may want to add a touch of coconut sugar at this point. Serve scattered with extra herbs.

TOFU ADOBO

Cooking meat with vinegar is the traditional "adobo" method of cooking in the Philippines. We've swapped the meat for tofu, and it's so good you'll want a double portion.

PREP TIME: 10 MINS · COOK TIME: 50 MINS

1¼ lb **extra firm tofu**

5 cloves of **garlic**, sliced

1 tablespoon **rice bran oil**

2 cups **vegetable stock**

3 tablespoons **tamari**

3 tablespoons **coconut vinegar**

3 teaspoons **coarsely ground black peppercorns**

3 **bay leaves**

5½ oz **green snap beans**, trimmed

1 teaspoon **coconut sugar**

1 teaspoon **cornstarch**

2 **scallions**, chopped

1. Heat the oven to 425°F.

2. Slice the tofu about ½ inch thick and cut each piece in half. Let stand on a plate lined with paper towels to absorb the excess water for about an hour. Then place the tofu on a baking pan lined with a sheet of nonstick parchment paper. Roast in the hot oven for about 30 minutes, turning the tofu over halfway so it is browned all over.

3. While the tofu is browning, heat a large pan and cook the garlic in the oil for a minute. Add the stock, tamari, vinegar, pepper, and bay leaves. Bring to a boil, then simmer for about 20 minutes until the sauce has reduced slightly and thickened.

4. Add the beans, sugar, and browned tofu and simmer for another 5 minutes. Mix the cornstarch with a little water and stir into the sauce. Cook for another minute to thicken the mixture. Serve scattered with chopped scallions with cauliflower rice on the side, if liked.

Serve this with rice or cauliflower couscous. The coconut vinegar can be swapped for rice vinegar.

ROASTED VEGETABLE MOLE

The vegetables given below are only suggestions—any combination would work well with the rich, dark, mole sauce. This sauce is a labor of love, and the praise you will receive will be totally worth it. Any leftover sauce can be frozen for use later.

PREP TIME: 30 MINS · SOAK TIME: 30 MINS · COOK TIME: 50 MINS

FOR THE MOLE

1 oz **dried ancho chiles**

2 large **tomatoes**, skinned

a pinch of **dried oregano**

1 tablespoon **sesame seeds**

1 tablespoon **pumpkin seeds**

1 tablespoon **walnuts**

a pinch of **ground cinnamon**

½ teaspoon **ground cumin**

½ teaspoon **fennel seeds**

3 **cloves**

6 **peppercorns**

1 **onion**, chopped

3 tablespoons **olive oil**

2 teaspoons **smoked paprika**

½ cup **raisins**

½ cup **flaked almonds**

vegetable stock, if needed

1¾ oz **sugar-free dark chocolate**

salt and **freshly ground black pepper**

FOR THE VEGETABLES

14 oz **butternut squash**

1 **cauliflower**

2 **red onions**

1 **red bell pepper**

kernels from 2 **cobs of corn**

2 tablespoons **olive oil**

salt and **freshly ground black pepper**

1. Heat the oven to 400°F.

2. Pour boiling water over the ancho chiles to cover and let stand for at least 30 minutes.

3. Coarsely chop the tomatoes and place them in a large bowl with the oregano. Lightly toast the seeds and nuts until golden brown, and add to the tomatoes.

4. Lightly toast the cinnamon, cumin, fennel seeds, cloves, and peppercorns until fragrant, then grind in a spice grinder, or in a mortar and pestle. Add to the bowl.

5. In a large skillet cook the onion in the olive oil for 10 minutes over medium heat. Add the smoked paprika, raisins, and almonds. Continue to cook for 10 minutes, until the raisins have puffed up and the almonds are lightly toasted.

6. Drain the ancho chiles and discard the stalks, reserving the soaking liquid. Slice the chiles thinly and add to the pan along with the tomato and seed mixture. Stir well and cook for 10 minutes. Pour in about 1 cup of the chile soaking liquid or vegetable stock and bring to a simmer. Cook for 10 more minutes, or until you have a thick sauce.

7. Grate the chocolate into the sauce. Season well with salt and tip into a food processor or liquidizer. Blitz until smooth. At this point the sauce can be sieved for a smooth finish, but you may prefer a little texture.

8. Cut the squash into ¾-inch chunks. Separate the cauliflower into smaller florets. Cut the onions and bell pepper into wedges. Toss all the vegetables in a bowl with the corn and olive oil. Season well and spoon onto a baking pan. Cook in the oven for about 25 minutes.

9. Serve the roasted vegetables topped with the mole sauce.

This sauce would also go well with sweet potato quesadillas (see page 28). When in season, swap half the cauliflower for Romanesco.

CRAB SALAD
WITH COURCHAMPS SAUCE

We love Courchamps sauce because it uses the brown meat of the crab, which often goes to waste.

PREP TIME: 20 MINS

1¾ oz **arugula**

1 **fennel bulb**, shaved

5½ oz **asparagus spears**, cooked and cut into thin slices

1 tablespoon **lemon juice**

1 tablespoon **olive oil**

10½ oz **white crabmeat**

handful of **cress**, to serve

FOR THE SAUCE

7 oz **brown crabmeat**

3 **shallots**, finely chopped

3 tablespoons chopped **fresh tarragon**

3 tablespoons chopped **fresh parsley**

2 teaspoons **Dijon mustard**

1 teaspoon **tamari**

2 tablespoons **Sambuca**, or other **aniseed liqueur**

juice of ½ **lemon**

3 tablespoons **olive oil**

salt and **freshly ground black pepper**

1. Blitz together all the sauce ingredients until smooth. Season well.

2. Toss the arugula with the fennel, asparagus, lemon, and oil. Top with the white crabmeat and drizzle with the Courchamps sauce. Scatter with cress to serve.

LAMB, FIG & WALNUT TAGINE

Once you make this, you'll never fig-et about it. One to eat near a roaring fire, in the dead of winter.

PREP TIME: 15 MINS · COOK TIME: 2 HOURS 30 MINS

1¾ lb **lamb shoulder**, cut into ¾-inch dice

3 tablespoons **sunflower oil**

3 **onions** (**red** or **white**), each sliced into 4 large disks

1½ teaspoons **ground ginger**

2 teaspoons **ground cinnamon**

1 teaspoon **whole coriander seeds**, coarsely ground

2 teaspoons **ground cumin**

4 strips of **orange peel**

1 stick of **cinnamon**

2 teaspoons **raw honey**

2 cups **lamb** or **chicken stock**

12 **semidried figs**

16 **walnut halves**

salt and **freshly ground black pepper**

TO SERVE

fresh **cilantro leaves**

extra **walnuts**, crushed

a drizzle of **raw honey** (optional)

1. Heat the oven to 325°F.

2. Season the lamb with salt and black pepper. Heat the oil in a large Dutch oven over medium heat and brown the meat all over. Remove the lamb and set aside. Wipe out the pan if needed.

3. Place the onion slices across the bottom of the Dutch oven and set the meat on top. Sprinkle with all the ground spices. Place the orange peel and the cinnamon stick around the lamb. Drizzle with the honey.

4. Pour in about 2 cups stock—you want to add enough liquid to come about one-third of the way up the meat. Bring to a simmer on the stove, cover, then put into the oven and cook slowly for 2 hours. Add the figs and walnuts and cook for another 20 to 30 minutes.

5. Remove from the oven and serve scattered with cilantro leaves and crushed walnuts, and drizzled with honey, if using.

RABBIT & PRUNES

Rabbit is an underrated lean and healthy meat. A true taste of the season of fall. Ask your butcher to cut your rabbit into chunks for you.

PREP TIME: 15 MINS · SOAK TIME: 30 MINS · COOK TIME: 1 HOUR 50 MINS

12 **prunes**

3 tablespoons **brandy**

2 tablespoons **olive oil**

2 **rabbits**, cut into chunks

3½ oz **bacon lardons**

1 **leek**, finely chopped

1 stalk of **celery**, finely chopped

15 small **shallots** or **pearl onions**

1 sprig **thyme**

1 **bay leaf**

1 cup **red wine**

2 cups **chicken stock**

1 tablespoon **Dijon mustard**

2 teaspoons **arrowroot** (optional)

2 tablespoons chopped **fresh parsley**

salt and **freshly ground black pepper**

1. Soak the prunes in the brandy for at least 30 minutes.

2. Heat the oil in a large pan, then brown the rabbit pieces. Remove them from the pan and set aside. Add the bacon, leek, and celery to the pan and cook over low heat for 10 minutes.

3. Add the shallots and herbs along with the red wine. Bring to a boil, scraping the bottom of the pan with a wooden spoon. Add the stock and mustard, along with the prunes and any soaking liquid. Return the rabbit pieces to the pan. Cover and let simmer for about 1 hour 30 minutes, or until the rabbit is tender.

4. If your sauce is not looking thick enough, mix the arrowroot with a few tablespoons of water until smooth. Add to the rabbit sauce and stir to blend. Cook for a few minutes, until the sauce has thickened. Season, and serve scattered with chopped parsley.

PORK, APPLE & CHILE

We're not telling any porky pies (lies)—this slow-cooked stew will knock your socks off.

PREP TIME: 10 MINS · COOK TIME: 1 HOUR 50 MINS

¼ cup **canola oil**, divided

1 **onion**, finely chopped

3 cloves of **garlic**, crushed

2¼ lb **pork for stew** (**leg** or **shoulder**), cut into ¾-inch cubes

1 **bay leaf**

3 to 4 sprigs of **thyme**

1 to 2 sprigs of **rosemary**

2 **apples**, peeled, cored, and sliced

1 **hot red chile**, seeded and sliced

about 1¾ cups **hard cider**

1 cup **chicken stock**

salt and **freshly ground black pepper**

1. Heat the oven to 350°F.

2. Heat 2 tablespoons of oil in a nonstick skillet over low heat. Add the onion and gently fry until it's soft and translucent. Add the garlic and cook for a further minute or so, until really fragrant.

3. Transfer the onion and garlic to a Dutch oven, then add another tablespoon of oil to the skillet. Raise the heat to medium and, when the oil is hot, add the pork in batches and brown it. Place the browned pork in the Dutch oven, along with the herbs, salt, and pepper.

4. When you've finished browning the pork, add the final tablespoon of oil to the skillet (if needed), and brown the apples for about 5 minutes. Halfway through cooking, add the chile, stirring it through the apples, then add the mixture to the Dutch oven.

5. Deglaze the skillet with ½ cup of the hard cider and add the stock. Bring the combined liquids to a boil. Pour this over the pork and apple and top off the casserole with the remaining hard cider until everything is just covered with liquid. Cover and cook in the oven for 90 minutes.

6. Remove from the oven and use a slotted spoon to scoop the meat and apples onto a warm plate. Bring the sauce to a boil and reduce by about one-third, or until the sauce has thickened and coats the back of a spoon. Return the meat and apples to the Dutch oven, stir through, and serve.

BIRYANI

¼ cup **cashews**, soaked in plenty of **cold water** for 4 hours

½ cup **raisins**, soaked in **hot water** for at least 30 minutes

a pinch of **saffron**, soaked in 2 tablespoons **hot almond milk** for at least 30 minutes

1 head of **cauliflower**

2 tablespoons **coconut oil**

1 teaspoon **cumin seeds**

4 **cardamom pods**, bruised

3 **cloves**

1 **star anise**

1 **bay leaf**

1 × ¾-inch stick of **cinnamon**

a pinch of **ground mace**

2 cloves of **garlic**, crushed

1 × ¾-inch piece of **ginger**, grated

½ teaspoon **ground turmeric**

a large pinch of **dried chile flakes**

1 teaspoon **garam masala**

2 **parsnips**, peeled and cut into small chunks

7 oz **butternut squash**, peeled and cut into small chunks

3½ oz **green snap beans**, trimmed and cut into 1-inch pieces

10 **radishes**, halved

3½ oz **mushrooms**, quartered

1¼ cups **cooked chickpeas**

½ cup **cooked spinach**, chopped

salt and **freshly ground black pepper**

1 tablespoon each chopped **fresh cilantro** and **fresh mint**, to serve

The ingredient list looks very long here, but it's mainly the array of spices used to make the dish fragrant. A good-quality curry paste could be used instead. Feel free to substitute the vegetables with whatever you have on hand.

**PREP TIME: 30 MINS · SOAK TIME: 4 HOURS
COOK TIME: 30 MINS**

1. Blitz the cauliflower florets into tiny pieces in a food processor, or use a grater, and set aside.

2. Add the cumin seeds, cardamom pods, cloves, star anise, bay leaf, cinnamon, and mace to the oil remaining in the pan, and cook for a few minutes over gentle heat. Add the garlic and ginger, along with the turmeric, chile flakes, and garam masala and cook for another minute.

3. Tip in the parsnips and squash. Stir well and cover. Let cook for 10 minutes, then add the beans, radishes, and mushrooms. Cover and cook for a further 5 minutes.

4. Add the chickpeas and spinach, along with the blitzed cauliflower rice and the drained cashews. Turn up the heat and cook for 5 minutes, stirring well to prevent sticking.

5. Drain the raisins and squeeze out any excess moisture. Add to the cauliflower-rice mixture along with the saffron milk. Season well and fold through. Cover and let stand for 10 minutes.

6. Serve scattered with lots of chopped cilantro and mint.

Arti, a splendid accountant at LEON, makes her biryani with chopped oven chips (yes) as a weeknight shortcut, with kernel corn, chopped tomatoes, bell peppers, and pomegranate seeds.

GRILLED OCTOPUS SALAD

The potato salad served with the octopus is fab on its own or as an accompaniment to any summer lunch.

PREP TIME: 20 MINS · COOK TIME: 1 HOUR 30 MINS

2¼ lb **octopus**, cleaned

2 tablespoons **olive oil**, divided

2 **red chiles**

10 cloves of **garlic**, 8 peeled and left whole, 2 crushed

4 sprigs of **fresh flat-leaf parsley**

1 lb 2 oz **new potatoes**

3 **red onions**, finely chopped

3 tablespoons **apple cider vinegar**

2 teaspoons **coconut sugar**

5½ oz **sugar snap peas**, trimmed and thinly sliced

1 cup **fava beans**, cooked

¾ cup **peas**, cooked

2 tablespoons **extra virgin olive oil**

3 tablespoons snipped **fresh chives**

2½ cups **pea shoots** or **watercress**

salt and **freshly ground black pepper**

1. Ask your fish dealer to prepare and clean the octopus tentacles and head for you. Wash well under cold running water.

2. Heat 1 tablespoon of olive oil in a pan or pressure cooker until very hot. Add the chiles, whole garlic cloves, and parsley, along with the cleaned octopus. Stir for a minute and cover the pan tightly. If using a pressure cooker, cook for about 40 minutes, if not, cook over low heat for about 1 hour, or until the octopus flesh is tender. Let cool in the cooking juices.

3. Cook the new potatoes in lots of boiling salted water, then drain and let stand until cool enough to handle. Meanwhile, cook the onions in the remaining tablespoon of olive oil for 20 minutes, until the onions are soft. Add the crushed garlic, vinegar, and sugar and mix well. Turn up the heat and reduce the liquid to a syrup.

4. Slice the potatoes when they are cool enough to handle and fold into the onions. Add the sugar snap peas, fava beans, and peas. Drizzle with the extra virgin olive oil and fold together. Season well, scatter with the chives, and spoon onto a serving dish with the pea shoots or watercress.

5. Separate the tentacles of the octopus and slice the head into strips. Heat a griddle or barbecue until very hot, and sear the octopus pieces until charred on both sides. Season and serve on top of the salad.

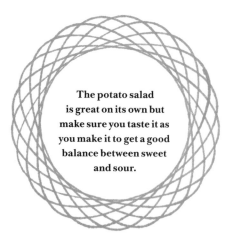

The potato salad is great on its own but make sure you taste it as you make it to get a good balance between sweet and sour.

JAMAICAN CURRY

To achieve an authentic taste, you should use Scotch bonnet chiles, but they can be very fiery. Leaving them whole in the curry for a limited time will give a milder result.

PREP TIME: 20 MINS · MARINATING TIME: OVERNIGHT · COOK TIME: 2 HOURS

3¼ lb **goat** or **lamb**, on the bone, cut into ¾-inch pieces

juice of 1 **lime**

2 teaspoons **fresh thyme leaves**

1 teaspoon **salt**

2 tablespoons **coconut oil**

2 teaspoons **coconut sugar**

2 **onions**, chopped

1 **red bell pepper**, chopped

1 to 2 **Scotch bonnet chiles**

3 cloves of **garlic**, crushed

1 × ¾-inch piece of **ginger**, grated

3 tablespoons **Jamaican curry powder**

5 **allspice berries**

½ × 14 oz can of **diced tomatoes**

2 cups **chicken stock**

3 **sweet potatoes**, peeled and cut into ¾-inch chunks

1 teaspoon **apple cider vinegar**

salt and **freshly ground black pepper**

1. Toss the goat or lamb pieces with the lime juice, thyme leaves, and salt to coat, and let marinate for a few hours or overnight. Drain and pat dry with paper towels before cooking.

2. Heat the oil in a large pan and add the marinated pieces of meat. Sprinkle with the sugar and stir-fry for a few minutes, to brown. Remove from the pan and reduce the heat. Add the onions, red bell pepper, chiles, garlic, and ginger. Cook for 5 minutes, then add the curry powder and allspice berries. Stir well to combine, then tip in the tomatoes.

3. Turn up the heat and return the meat to the pan with the chicken stock. Cover and let simmer for about 1 hour. Add the sweet potatoes and cook for a further 40 minutes, or until the potatoes are tender. Season well and add a little vinegar before serving.

We serve ours with an avocado salsa (made of chopped avocado, lime juice, and cilantro, seasoned with salt and pepper) as a great alternative to yogurt when the curry gets too hot.

GRILLED SARDINES WITH AN OLIVE & CAPER STUFFING

The almond, caper, and olive stuffing would also work well with chicken or squid.

PREP TIME: 20 MINS · COOK TIME: 15 MINS

8 **sardines**, trimmed and
    butterflied

1 teaspoon **olive oil**

½ **lemon**

2½ cups **arugula**

1¾ oz **piquillo peppers**

1 **fennel bulb**, shaved

1 **lemon**, cut into wedges

FOR THE STUFFING

2 tablespoons **golden raisins**

3 tablespoons **olive oil**

¾ cup **ground almonds**

1 clove of **garlic**, crushed

3 tablespoons **pine nuts**, toasted

15 **black olives**, coarsely chopped

3 **anchovy fillets**, chopped

2 tablespoons **capers**

3 tablespoons chopped **fresh
    parsley**

salt and **freshly ground black
    pepper**

1. To make the stuffing soak the golden raisins in very hot water. Heat the oil in a large nonstick skillet and toast the almonds with the garlic until lightly browned, stirring well so they are evenly toasted. Be careful not to burn the garlic.

2. Drain the golden raisins and add them to the almonds along with the pine nuts, olives, anchovies, and capers. Stir and cook for a few minutes over low heat. Remove from the heat and add the parsley. Season well.

3. Heat a griddle or broiler until very hot. Brush the sardine skins with a little oil and season well. Place skin-side down on the griddle (or skin-side up under the broiler), for 1 minute, then flip the fish over and cook the other side for another minute. Squeeze the juice of half a lemon over the fish. Place the fish on a warm dish and scatter with the almond stuffing.

4. To serve, toss the arugula with the piquillo peppers and fennel. Serve with the sardines and a wedge of lemon on the side.

SOUTHERN INDIAN
SPICED FISH

This is based on a recipe in *Spice*, by Christine Manfield. Jane used to make this when she lived in Samoa. It's so easy.

PREP TIME: 15 MINS · COOK TIME: 30 MINS

1 teaspoon **ground turmeric**

1 teaspoon **cayenne pepper**

½ teaspoon **ground white pepper**

½ teaspoon **salt**

1½ lb **hake fillets**, skinned (or **other white fish**)

3 tablespoons **canola oil**, divided

1 × ¾-inch piece of **ginger**, finely grated

3 **cardamom pods**, crushed

3 **onions**, sliced

3 cloves of **garlic**, crushed

4 **green chiles**, sliced

1 teaspoon **ground coriander**

¾ cup **fish stock**

1¾ cups **coconut milk**

2 tablespoons **mustard seeds**

2 sprigs of **curry leaves**

salt and **freshly ground black pepper**

TO SERVE

juice of 1 **lime**

fresh cilantro leaves

1. Mix together the turmeric, cayenne, pepper, and salt. Cut the fish into large 1½-inch pieces and rub with the spice mixture. Heat 2 tablespoons of oil in a large nonstick skillet and cook the fish pieces for a minute on each side. Remove from the pan and set aside.

2. Put the ginger, cardamom, onions, garlic, and chiles into the pan and cook over low heat for 15 minutes, without browning. Add the ground coriander, fish stock, and coconut milk. Bring to a simmer and cook for 5 minutes. Return the fish to the pan and cook gently for 5 minutes or until the fish is just cooked (the length of time will depend on the thickness of the fillets).

3. Heat the remaining tablespoon of oil in another pan and add the mustard seeds and curry leaves. When the seeds start to pop, pour the contents of the pan into the coconut sauce and stir to combine.

4. Finish with a squeeze of lime juice then scatter with cilantro leaves to serve.

CHERMOULAH MONKFISH

This North African spice blend is fantastic with fish. You'd traditionally use a chermoulah seasoning on lamb or chicken, but monkfish is so meaty that it can stand up to the bold flavor.

**PREP TIME: 15 MINS · MARINATING TIME: OVERNIGHT
COOK TIME: 25 MINS**

1¼ lb **monkfish tails**

1 tablespoon **olive oil**

2 **cardamom pods**, crushed

1 clove of **garlic**, crushed

1 × ¾-inch piece of **ginger**, grated

4 large **tomatoes**, skinned and chopped

½ cup **cooked Puy lentils**

½ cup **fish stock**

2 tablespoons chopped **fresh cilantro**

2 cups **watercress**

salt and **freshly ground black pepper**

FOR THE CHERMOULAH MARINADE

1 teaspoon **ground coriander**

1 teaspoon **ground cumin**

1 teaspoon **ground fennel seeds**

juice of ½ **lemon**

1 tablespoon **red wine vinegar**

1 clove of **garlic**, crushed

1 **red chile**, finely chopped

1 teaspoon **coconut sugar**

1 teaspoon **smoked paprika**

1. Mix together all the marinade ingredients. Place the monkfish in the marinade and let stand in the refrigerator for a few hours or overnight.

2. Heat a tablespoon of olive oil in a pan and add the cardamom, garlic, and ginger. Cook for 2 minutes over low heat, then add the chopped tomatoes. Turn the heat up and cook for 10 minutes, until you have a thick sauce. Add the lentils and fish stock, stir well, and bring to a simmer. Cook for a few minutes, then season well and stir in the fresh cilantro. Keep the sauce warm while you cook the fish.

3. Heat a griddle until very hot. Remove the monkfish from its marinade and cook for about 5 minutes on the griddle, making sure it is browned on all sides.

4. When the tails are firm to touch, remove from the griddle and let rest for a few minutes. The cooking time will depend on the size and thickness of the tails.

5. Slice the fish into ¾-inch pieces and arrange in a dish on top of the sauce. Scatter with watercress to serve.

BRAISED CLAMS, MUSSELS, FENNEL, LEEKS & 'NDUJA

Chorizo can be used instead of 'nduja (a spicy, spreadable sausage), but it won't melt into the sauce the way the soft Calabrian paste will.

PREP TIME: 10 MINS · COOK TIME: 15 MINS

2 **shallots**, sliced

2 **leeks**, sliced

2 bulbs of **fennel**, sliced

4 cloves of **garlic**, crushed

3 tablespoons **'nduja**

3 tablespoons **olive oil**

2¼ lb **mussels**, cleaned

2¼ lb **clams**

½ cup **white wine**

2 tablespoons chopped **fresh parsley**

1. Cook the shallots, leeks, fennel, and garlic, with the 'nduja, in the olive oil for about 2 minutes. The 'nduja should dissolve on cooking.

2. Heat a large pan until very hot. Tip in the mussels and clams and pour in the white wine. Cover immediately and shake the pan. Cook for a few minutes, until all the shells start to open (discarding any shells that do not open). Immediately empty the shellfish into a colander over a bowl to collect the cooking liquor.

3. Pour the liquor into the fennel mixture and bring to a simmer. Cook for 5 minutes, then stir in the mussels and clams. Serve scattered with plenty of chopped parsley.

BEAN & SAUERKRAUT SOUP

This soup is a little unusual, but will soon become something you make all the time. It's long been known that sauerkraut is oh-so-good for you. It aids digestion, is full of good bacteria, and has even been said to have cancer-fighting properties.

**PREP TIME: 20 MINS · SOAKING TIME: OVERNIGHT
COOK TIME: 1 HOUR**

1 cup **cranberry beans**, soaked overnight in lots of **cold water**

10 cloves of **garlic**, 6 peeled but left whole; 4 peeled and crushed

2 **bay leaves**

4 **cherry tomatoes**

1 lb 2 oz **kohlrabi**, peeled and diced

2 tablespoons **olive oil**

2 **onions**, diced

2 teaspoons **caraway seeds**, crushed

1 tablespoon **paprika**

2 cups drained **sauerkraut**, rinsed

2 tablespoons chopped **fresh parsley**

salt and **freshly ground black pepper**

1. Drain the beans and place in a pan. Cover with about a quart of water and add the whole cloves of garlic, bay leaves, and tomatoes. Bring to a boil, then simmer for about 40 minutes, making sure the beans are always covered with plenty of water.

2. Add the diced kohlrabi to the pan and simmer for another 20 minutes, or until the kohlrabi is cooked. Remove the bay leaves and mash the bean and kohlrabi mixture coarsely with a potato masher. Take out a large cupful of the mixture, blend it, and return it to the beans. Stir well and season.

3. While the beans are cooking, heat the oil in a pan and cook the onions for 10 minutes. Add the crushed cloves of garlic and caraway seeds and cook for a minute. Turn up the heat and stir in the paprika and sauerkraut. Stir-fry for a few minutes, then tip all the ingredients into the bean pan. Add a little water to the onion pan and scrape the contents out into the soup pan.

4. Stir everything together, adding a little water or vegetable stock if the soup is too thick. Check the seasoning, and serve scattered with parsley.

BITS ON THE SIDE

POTATO FOCACCIA

A light, fluffy, and magnificently hearty loaf based on a traditional Pugliese bread. This recipe has quite a few steps and takes patience to make, but the rewards couldn't be more worth the effort. We think it's best served sliced, toasted, and with some of our top dips (see page 78).

PREP TIME: 20 MINS · RISE TIME: 40 TO 60 MINS · COOK TIME: 45 MINS

10½ oz **baking potatoes**

2 × ¼-oz sachets of **active dry yeast**

1 tablespoon **raw honey**

½ cup **tepid water**

1 tablespoon **psyllium husks**

1 teaspoon **ground chia seeds**

1 teaspoon **ground flaxseeds**

1¾ cups **cold water**

2 **egg whites**

¼ cup **olive oil**, divided

10 **cherry tomatoes**, halved

1 tablespoon chopped **fresh rosemary**

sea salt

FOR THE FLOUR MIX

1 cup **sorghum flour**

1 cup **millet flour**

1 cup **tapioca flour**

1¾ cup **polenta**

¾ cup **arrowroot**

2 teaspoons **baking powder**

1 teaspoon **vitamin C powder**

1 teaspoon **salt**

1. Boil the baking potatoes in their skins until tender.

2. Place all the flour mix ingredients in a large bowl. Mix the yeast with the honey and ½ cup of tepid water. Mix the psyllium husks and ground seeds with the cold water.

3. When the potatoes are cool enough to handle, remove the skins and push the potatoes through a potato ricer into the bowl containing the flour. Rub together.

4. Whisk the egg whites until just holding soft peaks. Add the yeast mixture to the psyllium mixture and stir. Pour into the flour mixture along with the egg whites and mix together until well combined. You should have a very wet, sticky dough. Mix in half of the olive oil and let rise for 20 minutes.

5. Transfer the dough to a baking pan lined with nonstick parchment paper and spread it out, using your fingers, into a rough oblong ¾ inch deep.

6. Top with the cherry tomatoes, skin-side up, and sprinkle with the rosemary and sea salt. Let stand in a warm place until doubled in size, about 20 to 40 minutes.

7. Heat the oven to 425°F.

8. Drizzle the focaccia with the remaining olive oil and bake for 20 to 25 minutes, or until well browned and cooked through. Transfer to a rack and let cool completely before slicing.

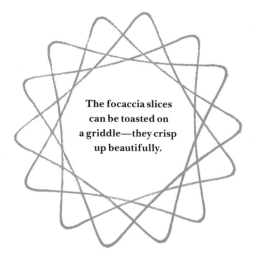

The focaccia slices can be toasted on a griddle—they crisp up beautifully.

 (NF) (V)

CORNBREAD

This is another recipe from our mates Meleni and Rob, who advise us at LEON about our nutrition. You can also add whole corn kernels for a bit of extra texture.

PREP TIME: 15 MINS · COOK TIME: 30 MINS

½ cup **coconut oil**, melted

1 cup **polenta**

1½ cups **masa harina**

2 teaspoons **baking powder**

1 teaspoon **sweet paprika**

1 teaspoon **smoked paprika**

a large pinch of **salt**

2 **eggs**

2½ tablespoons **rice malt syrup**

1 cup **coconut milk**

corn kernels from 1 cob (optional for texture)

1. Heat the oven to 400°F.

2. Using a little coconut oil, grease an 8-inch square cake pan and line it with nonstick parchment paper.

3. Mix together the dry ingredients. Separately, beat the eggs lightly together and add the rest of the oil, syrup, and coconut milk. Beat to combine.

4. Pour the wet ingredients into the dry and stir just to combine. Add the corn kernels, if using. Do not overmix. Pour the batter into the pan and bake in the oven for 25 to 30 minutes. Serve warm or at room temperature.

PITA PAN

3½ tablespoons **ground psyllium husks**

2½ cups **water**

1 lb 10 oz **gluten-free bread flour**

3 tablespoons **sesame seeds**

1 tablespoon **ground fennel seeds**

1 tablespoon **raw honey**

1 tablespoon **salt**

2 tablespoons **instant yeast**

3 **eggs**

1 tablespoon **white wine vinegar**

½ cup **olive oil**

It'd be a real pity if you couldn't have pita any more just because of gluten. Don't be turned off by the psyllium husks. It's much more natural than it sounds. Made from plant husks, it helps bind the ingredients in gluten-free bread and it's great for digestion. We prefer it to xanthan gum, which sometimes doesn't agree with people's digestion.

PREP TIME: 20 MINS · RISE TIME: 20 MINS
COOK TIME: 45 MINS

1. Mix the psyllium powder with 1¼ cups water. Set aside to thicken.

2. Tip the flour and seeds into a mixing bowl. Add the honey and salt to one side of the bowl and the yeast to the other. Crack the eggs into the center of the flour, then add the vinegar, olive oil, and the psyllium mixture. Combine to form a soft dough. Gradually add the remaining water (you may not need it all). The dough should be soft and slightly sticky.

3. Place on a floured surface and knead for a few minutes to form a smooth dough. Put back into the bowl, cover, and let rest for 1½ hours, until doubled in size.

4. Set the oven to 425°F and place 3 sturdy baking pans in the oven to heat up.

5. Dust your work surface with flour. Divide the dough into 12 equal pieces and shape each one into a ball. Roll or press the pieces into oval shapes about ¼ inch thick.

6. Carefully remove the hot baking pans from the oven and dust with a little flour. Lay 4 pitas on each pan and bake for 10 to 12 minutes, until puffed up and cooked through. The pitas should have a slight color to them. Remove from the oven and wrap in a clean dish towel to help keep them soft until you are ready to serve.

Try these pitas with the fava bean purée on page 68.

ZUCCHINI SALAD

It doesn't get much fresher than this.

PREP TIME: 10 MINS · STAND TIME: 20 MINS

5 **zucchini**

juice of ½ **lemon**

2 tablespoons chopped **fresh mint**

2 tablespoons **olive oil**

1 **red chile**, chopped

1 tablespoon finely chopped **black olives**

salt and **freshly ground black pepper**

1. Finely julienne or grate the zucchini. Place in a colander and add about ½ teaspoon of salt. Mix together and let stand for at least 20 minutes.

2. Squeeze out any excess moisture from the zucchini, then mix with the rest of the ingredients before serving.

PARSNIP QUINOA WITH HAZELNUTS, MINT & APRICOTS

Up your quinoa game with this parsnip-pimped version.

PREP TIME: 10 MINS · COOK TIME: 25 MINS

9 oz **parsnips**, peeled and finely chopped

4 **dried apricots**, finely chopped

1 cup **quinoa**

1 tablespoon **olive oil**

2 tablespoons **hazelnuts**, crushed

2 tablespoons chopped **fresh mint**

1 tablespoon **lemon juice**

salt and **freshly ground black pepper**

1. Place the parsnips and apricots in a pan. Cover with water and simmer for about 10 minutes, or until the parsnips are tender. Drain, reserving the cooking liquid in a large measuring cup. Make up to 1¼ cups with water.

2. Rinse the quinoa under cold running water and let drain. Heat the oil in a pan and add the drained quinoa. Stir-fry for a minute and season. Add the 1¼ cups of liquid and bring to a simmer. Cover and cook for 15 minutes. Add the parsnips and apricots, then cover the pan and let stand in a warm place for at least another 15 minutes.

3. Stir in the hazelnuts, mint, and lemon juice. Season well before serving.

MARINATED EGGPLANT WEDGES

Live life on the wedge.

PREP TIME: 10 MINS · COOK TIME: 25 MINS

3 large **eggplants**, peeled with a paring knife

3 tablespoons **olive oil**

3 tablespoons **balsamic vinegar**

1 tablespoon **raw honey**

2 teaspoons **paprika**

3 cloves of **garlic**, minced

3 **red chiles**, seeded and chopped

1 tablespoon **mint**, chopped

2½ oz **arugula**

¼ cup **toasted pine nuts**

extra virgin olive oil, for drizzling

salt and **freshly ground black pepper**

1. Heat the oven to 350°F.

2. Cut the eggplants in half to make two shorter cylinders. Cut each cylinder into 8 to 10 wedges.

3. Mix together the oil, vinegar, honey, and paprika. Toss the eggplant wedges in this marinade and season well. Let marinate for about 30 minutes.

4. Tip the eggplant wedges onto a baking pan lined with nonstick parchment paper and place in the oven for about 20 minutes, or until they are just tender. Sprinkle with the garlic and chile. Return to the oven for another 5 minutes then set aside to cool.

5. To serve, toss the eggplant wedges with the mint and arugula and scatter with the pine nuts. Drizzle with extra virgin olive oil to serve.

PANISSE

These are a French chickpea version of polenta chips. Serve with plenty of sea salt and freshly ground black pepper.

PREP TIME: 5 MINS · COOK TIME: 20 MINS

3¼ cups **water**

½ teaspoon **ground fennel seeds**

1 teaspoon finely chopped **fresh rosemary**

½ teaspoon crushed **garlic**

a pinch of **chile flakes**

2 teaspoons **olive oil**

½ teaspoon **salt**

2 cups **gram flour**, sifted

canola oil, for frying

1. Pour the water into a pan and add the fennel seeds, rosemary, garlic, chile flakes, olive oil, and salt. Heat to a simmer and gradually stir in the sifted gram flour to avoid getting lumps. Beat together, then stir constantly with a wooden spoon for about 10 minutes over low heat.

2. The mixture should be smooth. If not, press it through through a sieve. Pour it out onto a greased baking pan. Smooth with a metal spatula until ½ inch deep and let cool. Cut into short strips about ¾ × 1½ inches in size.

3. Heat about ¾ inch of oil in a skillet and fry the panisse fingers for a few minutes, until lightly browned and crisp all over. Drain on paper towels before serving.

SOCCA

This thin chickpea pancake from Nice is great to serve with drinks. An anchovy mayonnaise or tapenade alongside some braised greens would make a tasty accompaniment. We have cooked our socca in the oven, but it can be made directly on the stove or under a broiler. The secret is to cook it as thin as possible on a hot surface so the results are very crisp.

**PREP TIME: 10 MINS · STAND TIME: 2 HOURS
COOK TIME: 25 MINS**

2 cups **gram flour**, sifted

1 teaspoon **salt**

a pinch of **ground cumin**

1 teaspoon finely chopped **fresh rosemary**

1 cup **water**

2 tablespoons **olive oil**, plus extra for cooking

1. Heat the oven to 425°F.

2. Place the flour in a large bowl with the salt, cumin, and rosemary. Add the water, beating until you have a smooth batter the consistency of light cream. Beat in the olive oil. Let stand for at least 2 hours (it can also be made up to this point the night before).

3. Place a cast-iron skillet in a hot oven for about 10 minutes. Carefully remove from the oven and drizzle with a tablespoon of olive oil. Whisk the batter and pour in enough to cover the bottom of the pan in a thin layer. Return it to the oven for about 10 minutes, or until the edges and top are browning.

4. Slide the socca out of the pan onto a board and cut into coarse pieces to serve. Repeat with the rest of the batter and break into pieces to serve.

Socca can be used as a pizza crust but it will lose its crispiness as the toppings start to seep through.

BITS ON THE SIDE

CARROT TOP PESTO & CARROTS

1¼ lb **carrots**, with fresh-looking green tops

3 tablespoons **olive oil**, plus 1 tablespoon

1 teaspoon **raw honey**

1 small bunch of **fresh basil**

2 tablespoons **pine nuts**, toasted

1 clove of **garlic**, crushed

1 tablespoon **lemon** juice

salt and **freshly ground black pepper**

Jane has become slightly obsessed with "vegetable offal"—the bits that we throw away but that are actually truly marvelous. You could also try making chips from vegetable peel, or sautéeing cauliflower leaves or beet tops.

PREP TIME: 10 MINS · COOK TIME: 40 MINS

1. Heat the oven to 325°F.

2. Cut the tops off the carrots, rinse, and chop coarsely.

3. Cut the carrots in half lengthwise and toss with salt and pepper and 1 tablespoon of the olive oil. Place on a baking pan and drizzle with a little honey. Place in the oven for about 40 minutes, or until the carrots are tender.

4. Place the carrot tops in a food processor with the basil, pine nuts, and garlic. Blitz to a coarse paste and transfer to a bowl. Add the lemon juice and the 3 tablespoons of olive oil. Season the pesto to taste.

5. Arrange the carrots on a serving dish and drizzle with the pesto.

SQUASH & SAGE

Fragrant sage and sweet squash—you'd be hard-pressed to find something so wholly autumnal as this.

PREP TIME: 10 MINS · COOK TIME: 10 MINS

14 oz **butternut squash**

3 tablespoons **olive oil**

2 cloves of **garlic**, thinly sliced

20 **fresh sage leaves**

2 tablespoons toasted **pine nuts**

a drizzle of **pumpkin seed oil**
   (optional)

salt and **freshly ground black
   pepper**

1. Using a speed peeler or mandoline slicer, shave thin strips from the squash into a bowl. No need to peel it first.

2. Heat the oil in a large pan and cook the garlic and sage for 2 minutes without browning the garlic. Remove with a slotted spoon.

3. Tip the squash into the pan and turn up the heat. Cook for 3 minutes, stirring well. Cover, then turn the heat down low for 3 minutes or until the squash is just cooked. Season well.

4. Stir in the garlic, sage, and pine nuts and transfer to a serving dish. Drizzle with a little pumpkin seed oil, if you have it to serve.

PITTA DI PATATE

This onion and potato bread recipe was taught to Jane by a charming lady, Gianna Greco, who has a cookery school in Lecce, Puglia. The original had some cheese and bread crumbs, but we tried it with toasted almonds and it was a roaring success. It is generally served slightly warm as part of an antipasti spread.

PREP TIME: 15 MINS · COOK TIME: 1 HOUR 40 MINS

6 **onions**, halved and thinly sliced

2 tablespoons **olive oil**, plus extra for greasing and drizzling

about 1 cup **water**

3 tablespoons **tomato passata (or chopped** and **peeled tomatoes)**

3 tablespoons **salted capers**, soaked in **cold water**

1 tablespoon shredded **fresh basil**

2¼ lb **russet potatoes**

2 **eggs**, beaten

¾ cup **ground almonds**, divided

2 tablespoons chopped **fresh parsley**

2 tablespoons snipped **fresh chives**

salt and **freshly ground black pepper**

1. Heat the oven to 400°F.

2. Place the onions in a large shallow pan with the olive oil and cook over medium heat for about 10 minutes, without coloring. Add the water, bring to a simmer, and continue to cook gently for about 45 minutes. The longer you can cook the onions, the better flavor in the resulting dish.

3. Add the tomato passata and drained capers and cook for another 15 minutes. Stir in the basil.

4. While the onions are cooking, boil the potatoes in their skins until tender, then drain. When the potatoes are cool enough to handle, peel off the skins.

5. Pass the potatoes through a potato ricer into a large bowl and beat in the eggs. Lightly toast half the ground almonds and add to the bowl with the herbs. Season the potato mix very well.

6. Grease a 8½-inch square baking dish with a little oil. Press half the potato mixture into the bottom of the dish to form a smooth layer. Top with the slow-cooked onions and any juices they may have. Add a final layer of potato and smooth down with a metal spatula. Sprinkle with the rest of the ground almonds and drizzle with lots of olive oil.

7. Bake in the oven for about 30 minutes, or until the top is golden brown. Cut into squares to serve.

FERMENTED BEETS & FENNEL

1 quart **water**

2 tablespoons **sea salt**

3 to 4 **beets**

1 **bulb of fennel**

½ teaspoon **fennel seeds**

This comes from our friend Jonny Guest, who was responsible for the sauerkraut recipe in *Fast Vegetarian*. Remember to loosen the lid every day for the first week of fermentation, to remove any gas. This will save you from causing an explosion.

PREP TIME: 10 MINS · FERMENTING TIME: 2 WEEKS

1. Mix the water with the salt until completely dissolved.

2. Wash and scrub the beets, then top and tail and finely slice. Trim the fennel and finely slice.

3. In a clean 1-quart jar, layer alternately the beets and the fennel with a few fennel seeds. Press down firmly. Cover completely with the brine and secure the lid. The vegetables must stay submerged in the brine for the fermentation to be successful.

4. Let stand in a warm place for 2 weeks, loosening the lid every day for the first week, or until the vegetables are crunchy but have lost their "rawness" and have a nice sour taste.

PATRA

1 bunch of **collard greens**

2 tablespoons **rice bran oil**

1 tablespoon **mustard seeds**

1 tablespoon **sesame seeds**

2 **onions**, thinly sliced

a pinch of **asafetida**

FOR THE PASTE

1½ cups **gram flour**

2 teaspoons **ground coriander**

1 teaspoon **ground cumin**

1 tablespoon **sesame seeds**

ground chili powder, to taste

¾-inch piece of **ginger**, finely grated

2 **green chiles**, finely chopped

1 teaspoon **salt**

2 teaspoons **tamarind paste**

2 teaspoons **palm sugar**

2 tablespoons **rice bran oil**

½ cup **water**

These stuffed greens remind us of a jelly roll. You can steam the rolls, let them cool, and keep in the fridge for hours until you're ready to fry. Serve with chutneys and dal.

PREP TIME: 40 MINS · COOK TIME: 40 MINS

1. Separate the leaves of the collard greens and use a sharp knife to remove the thick part of the central rib.

2. Blend together all the paste ingredients in a food processor until you have a spreadable paste, adding more water if required.

3. Take 2 of the largest leaves and spread them out on a clean cloth or work surface. Spread a thin layer of the paste onto each leaf. Top with another leaf. Repeat the process until all the paste has been used. Roll up each pile into a long thin tube. Place in a steamer (you may have to cut the rolls in half to fit them in) and steam for 25 minutes, or until they are firm to the touch.

4. When cool, slice into disks about ¾ inch thick. Heat the oil in a large skillet. Add the mustard and sesame seeds. When the seeds start to pop, add the onions and asafetida. Cook for 5 minutes, then remove from the pan with a slotted spoon and set aside. Start browning the patra slices for a few minutes each side, adding more oil if needed. When all the patra slices are browned, toss together with the onions and seeds and serve.

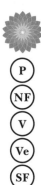

TRUFFLE PARSNIP FRIES

Keep your eyes on the fries. Seriously. If you're not careful, everyone'll steal 'em.

PREP TIME: 5 MINS · COOK TIME: 30 MINS

6 large **parsnips**, peeled

2 tablespoons **olive oil**

salt and **freshly ground black pepper**

TO FINISH

a drizzle of **truffle oil**

a sprinkle of **truffle salt**

2 tablespoons snipped **fresh chives**

1. Heat the oven to 375°F.

2. Cut the parsnips into chips or wedges about ½ inch thick. Toss with the olive oil to coat and then season. Place on a baking pan lined with nonstick parchment paper and cook in the oven for about 20 minutes. Check the parsnips, give the pan a shake. Put them back in the oven for an extra 10 minutes if they are not quite cooked.

3. Scoop the parsnips off of the pan and onto a serving dish. Drizzle with truffle oil and sprinkle with truffle salt and chives to serve.

We served these with a dollop of truffle honey, which goes so well with the sweet parsnips.

SWEET POTATO GRATIN

This gratin is great in all scenarios.

PREP TIME: 10 MINS · COOK TIME: 45 MINS

2¼ lb **sweet potatoes**, peeled

1 cup **unsweetened almond milk**

3 cloves of **garlic**, crushed

2 **red chiles**, chopped

2 tablespoons finely chopped **fresh rosemary**

1 teaspoon **arrowroot**

salt and **freshly ground black pepper**

1. Heat the oven to 325°F.

2. Thinly slice the sweet potatoes, season, and layer in a 10-inch gratin dish or similar shallow baking dish.

3. Heat the almond milk with the garlic, chiles, and rosemary and beat together. Simmer for a few minutes to reduce a little, then mix the arrowroot with a tablespoon of water and whisk into the liquid to make a sauce.

4. Season the sauce and pour evenly over the sweet potatoes. Cover the dish with foil or a lid and bake in the oven for about 40 minutes, or until the sweet potatoes are tender. Leave to cool slightly before serving.

BEET GRATIN

This vivid purple gratin is incredible with smoked fish or roast beef. A step in the right direction toward eating the rainbow.

PREP TIME: 10 MINS · COOK TIME: 55 MINS

2¼ lb **beets**

1 tablespoon **olive oil**

2 **shallots**, finely chopped

1 clove of **garlic**, crushed

1 tablespoon chopped **fresh savory**

1 tablespoon **crushed pink peppercorns**

2 tablespoons grated **horseradish**

½ cup **vegetable stock**

salt

1. Heat the oven to 325°F.

2. Peel and finely slice the beets.

3. Heat the olive oil in a pan and add the shallots. Cook over low heat for 10 minutes. Stir in the garlic, savory, peppercorns, and horseradish. Cook for a minute, then add the stock. Bring to a boil, then simmer for 5 minutes.

4. Add the beets and season with salt. Mix well and place in a 10-inch gratin dish or similar shallow baking dish baking dish in layers. Cover tightly with foil, place in the oven, and cook for about 40 minutes, or until the beets are tender. Leave to cool slightly before serving.

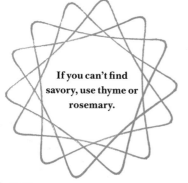

If you can't find savory, use thyme or rosemary.

CORN TORTILLAS & DIPS

Masa harina is a traditional Mexican flour made from ground corn kernels. Perfect for taco night, or try baking them with a little oil to make your own tortilla chips.

PREP TIME: 15 MINS · REST TIME: 30 MINS · COOK TIME: 30 MINS

1¼ cups **masa harina**

1 tablespoon **olive oil**

¾ cup **hot water**

salt

1. Place the masa harina in a bowl with a pinch of salt. Stir in the oil, then slowly add the hot water until you have a smooth dough. Knead for a while to bring together. Add more masa if it's too sticky; more water if too dry.

2. Let rest for about 30 minutes. Divide into 10 balls and roll out into small tortillas. This can be done using a tortilla press or with a rolling pin. If using a tortilla press, place the flattened ball between 2 sheets of nonstick parchment paper and place in the press to flatten.

3. Cook each tortillas as soon as you have pressed it. Heat a nonstick skillet or cast-iron griddle until very hot, and cook each tortilla about 2 minutes either side, until lightly browned and toasted.

4. Serve warm, with tomatillo salsa and avocado dip (see below).

TOMATILLO SALSA

PREP TIME: 10 MINS

1 clove of **garlic**, crushed

4 **jalapeño peppers**, chopped

14 oz **tomatillos**, chopped (use skinned ripe tomatoes if tomatillos aren't available)

6 **scallions**, chopped

juice of ½ **lime**

1 teaspoon **maple syrup**

2 tablespoons chopped **fresh cilantro**

salt

1. Mix all the ingredients together in a bowl and season with salt. This should keep in a sealed container in the refrigerator for up to 3 days.

AVOCADO DIP

PREP TIME: 5 MINS

2 ripe **avocados**

1 clove of **garlic**

1 teaspoon **chipotle paste**

3 tablespoons **olive oil**

juice of ½ **lime**

salt and **freshly ground black pepper**

1. Blend all the ingredients together until smooth, then season to taste. This should keep in a sealed container in the refrigerator for a day.

ETHIOPIAN FLATBREAD

This injera flatbread is normally made by a longer fermentation method, but we've sped it up for convenience and the results are good. This is normally served with a dal-like stew. A kachumber salad (see page 254) would complete the meal.

PREP TIME: 15 MINS · REST TIME: 1 HOUR · COOK TIME: 30 MINS

1 tablespoon **active dry yeast**

¾ cup **warm water**

1 cup **teff flour**

½ teaspoon **baking powder**

1 teaspoon **apple cider vinegar**

½ cup **cold water**

rice bran oil, for greasing

salt

1. Blend the yeast with the warm water. Mix with the flour and set aside for an hour. Whisk in the baking powder, vinegar, salt, and cold water so you have a thin batter.

2. Heat a nonstick skillet or griddle. Grease the pan using a cloth or a piece of paper towel dipped in oil. Ladle a little of the batter onto the pan and spread out either by using the ladle or tilting the pan.

3. Cover the pan for a minute to steam, uncover, then cook for another 3 minutes. Repeat with the rest of the batter and serve.

RED LENTIL STEW

PREP TIME: 5 MINS · COOK TIME: 45 MINS

2 **onions**, chopped

2 tablespoons **rice bran oil**

¼ cup **berbere (Ethiopian spice mix)**

1 tablespoon grated **ginger**

2 cloves of **garlic**, crushed

1 cup **red lentils**, rinsed well

¼ cup **water**

1 teaspoon **salt**

1. In a large pan cook the onions in the oil for 10 minutes. Add the spice mixture, ginger, and garlic and cook for another 3 minutes.

2. Add the lentils and stir well to combine. Pour in the water and bring to a simmer, then cook for 30 minutes, until the lentils have gone slightly mushy. Season with the salt and serve with the Ethiopian flat bread.

SANDWICH BREAD

After many, many attempts, this is the one. Jane's been through a lot. She tried one, and thought she had nailed it. It rose beautifully, but when she cut into it there was nothing inside. Just a hole. She stuck with it, though, and this bread is the perfect proof of persistence. We love it toasted, or used in a bacon, lettuce and tomato sandwich.

PREP TIME: 10 MINS · RISE TIME: 45 TO 55 MINUTES · COOK TIME: 40 MINS

2½ cups **lukewarm water**

3 teaspoons **active dry yeast**

2 teaspoons **raw honey**

1 cup **millet flour**

1 cup **sorghum flour**

1 cup **chestnut flour**

¾ cup **quinoa flour**

1 teaspoon **salt**

2 tablespoons **psyllium husks**

3 tablespoons **ground chia seeds**

3 tablespoons **olive oil**, plus extra for greasing

1. Mix the water with the yeast and honey. Set aside for about 15 minutes.

2. In a large bowl mix together all the dry ingredients. Line a greased 1-pound loaf pan with nonstick baking parchment.

3. Add the olive oil to the yeast solution and mix it into the dry ingredients. Bring together to make a soft dough. Turn out onto a clean work surface and knead lightly for a few minutes, adding a little extra flour if required. Place in the lined pan and let stand until the loaf has doubled in size, about 30 to 40 minutes.

4. Heat the oven to 425°F.

5. Bake the loaf in the oven for about 40 minutes. If it browns too much on top, cover with foil.

6. Remove from the oven and let cool in the pan.

You can use regular gluten-free flour, but we made a mixture here that's more nutritious and tasty.

SPICED CHICKPEAS

These are a great little bar (or sofa) snack.

PREP TIME: 5 MINS · COOK TIME: 30 MINS

2 × 14 oz cans of **chickpeas**, drained

2 tablespoons **olive oil**

½ teaspoon **ground cumin**

1 teaspoon **freshly ground black pepper**

chili powder, to taste

½ teaspoon **smoked paprika**

salt

1. Heat the oven to 400°F.

2. Rinse the chickpeas well under cold running water, then drain and dry with clean dish towels or paper towels.

3. Put the chickpeas into a bowl and toss with the olive oil to coat. Mix together the rest of the ingredients and toss through the chickpeas.

4. Place on a baking pan lined with nonstick parchment paper and roast in the preheated oven for about 30 minutes, giving the pan a shake after 15 minutes. When the chickpeas are crisp, turn off the oven but leave them inside the oven to cool down before serving.

KACHUMBER SALAD

This is such a great go-to side salad. It lends itself to Indian, Middle Eastern, and European dishes. It's a total all-rounder.

PREP TIME: 10 MINS

9 oz **tomatoes**, chopped

1 **red onion**, finely chopped

¼ **cucumber**, peeled and chopped

1 teaspoon **cumin seeds**, toasted and ground

1 tablespoon chopped **fresh cilantro**

1 tablespoon chopped **fresh mint**

1 **green chile**, chopped

1 tablespoon **balsamic vinegar**

½ teaspoon **salt**

a pinch of **cayenne pepper**

1. Mix all the ingredients together in a bowl.

Mix the spiced chickpeas with some kachumber salad, crushed peanuts, and tortilla chips for a bhel puri type salad.

You can change the spicing on these chickpeas. Try them with Indian spices like garam masala, or Mexican spices like chili powder and coriander.

7

TREAT YOURSELF

———————

TROPICAL TRIFLE

A slightly boozy trip down Memory Lane. We've added a splash of Malibu to the custard because it's John's tropical tipple of choice. (He is largely from the 80s.) This dessert wibbles while you wobble.

PREP TIME: 15 MINS · CHILL TIME: A FEW HOURS · COOK TIME: 15 MINS

½ quantity **basic sponge cake recipe** (see page 262)

3 tablespoons **spiced rum**

1 **mango**, peeled and diced

¼ **pineapple**, peeled and diced

1¼ cups **coconut cream**

toasted **coconut pieces**

FOR THE JELLY

2 tablespoons **agar flakes**

½ cup **boiling water**

¼ cup **brown rice syrup**

1¾ cups **orange** or **blood orange juice**

FOR THE COCONUT CUSTARD

6 **egg yolks**

1 tablespoon **palm sugar**

2 teaspoons **cornstarch**

1¼ cups **coconut milk**

a splash of **Malibu**

FOR THE PASSION FRUIT CURD

7 **passion fruits**, divided

3 tablespoons **coconut oil**

¼ cup **coconut sugar**

1 **egg**

2 **egg yolks**

1. Cut the sponge cake into chunks and place in the bottom of a large glass trifle dish. Drizzle with the rum and top with the fruit. Place the coconut cream in a bowl in the fridge.

2. Heat the agar flakes with the water and syrup. Simmer for 2 minutes, until the flakes have dissolved. Stir in the orange juice. Let cool a little, then pour evenly over the fruit. Transfer the dish to the fridge to allow the agar and orange juice mixture to set into a jelly (this may take a few hours).

3. Whisk the egg yolks with the sugar and cornstarch until smooth. Heat the coconut milk until it is just about to boil. Pour onto the egg yolks and whisk to combine. Return the mixture to the pan and cook over very low heat until the custard is of a coating consistency, about 5 minutes. Add Malibu to taste, and set aside to cool.

4. Blitz the pulp from 5 of the passion fruits, then sieve to remove the seeds. Combine the juice with the coconut oil, sugar, eggs, and yolks in a pan. Whisk together and cook gently over low heat to thicken, about 5 minutes. Stir in the pulp and seeds from the 2 remaining passion fruit. Let cool.

5. Spread the passion fruit curd over the cold, set orange jelly layer and top with the custard. Whip the chilled coconut cream and spoon it on top of the trifle. Sprinkle with toasted coconut to serve.

Agar is made from seaweed, and we love it. If you only have gelatin on hand, you can substitute equal amounts, but remember it won't be vegetarian.

STICKY TOFFEE PUDDING

We've probably never encountered a soul who wouldn't put their hand up for a dish of sticky toffee pudding. It's all in the name. Sticky. Toffee. Pudding. And now "free-from friends" will put their hand up, too. This recipe is adapted from the Macrobiotic School near Jane's house in Totnes, Devon.

PREP TIME: 15 MINS · COOK TIME: 1 HOUR

FOR THE TOFFEE SAUCE

½ cup **maple syrup**

½ cup **rice malt syrup**

a small pinch of **sea salt**

¾ cup **nondairy cream**, such as **soy**

FOR THE PUDDING

12 **dates**, pitted and finely chopped

8 **dried apricots**, finely chopped

1 teaspoon **baking soda**

3 tablespoons **coconut oil**

½ cup **almond milk**

½ teaspoon **vanilla extract**

3 tablespoons **maple syrup**

2 tablespoons **date syrup**

1¾ cups **gluten-free self-rising flour**

1 teaspoon **baking powder**

1 cup **almond milk**

1 teaspoon **vanilla extract**

2 **egg yolks**

2 teaspoons **cornstarch**

2 tablespoons **coconut sugar**

1. Boil the maple syrup, rice malt syrup, and salt together until you get a thick syrup.

2. Add the cream and reduce by one-third to one-half, or until it tastes like toffee sauce.

3. Pour into a 1½-quart pudding basin or ovenproof bowl and let cool.

4. Put the dates, apricots, and baking soda into a bowl and add just enough boiling water to cover. Let stand for 30 minutes to soften.

5. Heat the oven to 350°F.

6. Mix all the wet ingredients together. Sift the self-rising flour and baking powder into a mixing bowl, add the wet ingredients, and stir until smooth. Add the soaked fruit (don't drain it).

7. Pour the batter evenly on top of the sauce in the baking dish and bake in the oven for about 30 minutes, or until a toothpick inserted in the center comes out clean. Serve with almond milk custard (see below).

ALMOND MILK CUSTARD

PREP TIME: 10 MINS · COOK TIME: 5 MINS

1. Bring the almond milk and vanilla extract to a boil.

2. In a bowl, mix the yolks, cornstarch, and sugar. Add the hot milk and whisk until it thickens. If it doesn't thicken enough, put it back into the pan and place on the stove over low heat for a few minutes. Pour the custard through a sieve before serving.

VICTORIA SPONGE CAKE

Put a spring in your step with this sponge cake.

PREP TIME: 10 MINS · COOK TIME: 30 MINS · CHILL TIME: 10 MINS

3½ sticks **soy margarine**

2 cups **coconut sugar**

5 tablespoons **brown rice syrup**

2 teaspoons **vanilla extract**

8 **eggs**

3½ cups **gluten-free self-rising flour**

2 teaspoons **baking powder**

4 teaspoons **modified tapioca starch** (or **baking fix**), optional

TO SERVE

1 serving **vanilla cashew cream** (see page 270)

1 cup **raspberries**, plus extra to decorate

a handful of assorted **edible flowers**

1 tablespoon **desiccated coconut**

1. Heat the oven to 325°F.

2. Cream together the soy margarine and the coconut sugar. Beat in the rice syrup and the vanilla extract. Add the eggs one by one, beating well after each addition.

3. Sift together the rest of the ingredients and fold them into the cake mixture. Pour into a 9½-inch cake pan lined with nonstick parchment paper and bake in the oven for about 30 minutes, or until a skewer inserted in the center of the cake comes out clean. Transfer to a cooling rack and let cool for 10 minutes, then remove from the pan to finish cooling.

4. Once cooled, spread the vanilla cashew cream onto one cake and top with the raspberries. Add the second sponge on top and decorate with extra raspberries, edible flowers, and a dusting of desiccated coconut to serve

RAW CASHEW "CHEESECAKE"

Have your raw no-bake cake and eat it, too. We recommend you use an 8-inch springform cake pan. This is a recipe from Jane's friend Carrie Allcot, who she used to work with. Carrie's not sure where the recipe came from, but we're so glad it's here. A real showstopper.

PREP TIME: 30 MINS · SOAK TIME: OVERNIGHT · FREEZE TIME: A FEW HOURS

FOR THE BASE
7 oz **soft dates**

1 cup **ground almonds**

2 teaspoons **date syrup**

1 oz **sugar-free dark chocolate**, grated

FOR THE FILLING
1¾ cups **raw cashews**, soaked overnight in lots of **cold water**

juice of 4 **lemons**

1 teaspoon **vanilla extract** (or seeds from a **vanilla bean**)

½ cup **coconut oil**, melted

¼ cup **raw honey**

¾ cup **raspberries**, plus extra to decorate

½ cup peeled cooked **beets**

1. To make the crust, finely chop the dates and mix with the almonds, date syrup, and chocolate. Line a 9½-inch cake pan with nonstick parchment paper and press the mixture into the bottom of the pan. (Using your fingers is easier.) Keep in the fridge until the filling is ready.

2. Drain the nuts very well and place in a food processor with the lemon juice, vanilla, melted coconut oil, and honey. Blend until very smooth. A powerful blender will achieve smoother results.

3. Divide the mixture into thirds. Blend one-third with the raspberries, one-third with the beets, and leave the final third plain.

4. Layer the 3 colored purées on top of the cake crust, or you could swirl them together, if you like. Place in the freezer to set. Serve decorated with extra berries.

Try mixing different fruits or vegetables with the cashew cream to get a different spectrum of color, for example, try blackberries and blueberries or avocados and kiwifruit.

TREAT YOURSELF

MANGO-GO

V
Ve
SF

Another one from Carrie Allcot. Man, go make this delightfully dense pudding cake. Make sure you check the packets of your dried fruit though, there can often be sneakily added sugar.

PREP TIME: 20 MINS · STAND TIME: OVERNIGHT · COOK TIME: 50 MINS

¾ cup **dried mango**

¾ cup **dried apricots**

1¼ cups **boiling water**

1½ teaspoons **baking soda,** divided

1¼ cups **rice flour**

1 cup ground **macadamia nuts**

1 teaspoon **ground cinnamon**

1 teaspoon **ground ginger**

1 teaspoon **baking powder**

1 **ripe banana**

¾ cup **melted coconut oil**

a few drops of **vanilla extract**

a few tablespoons of **almond milk**

2 **mangoes**, cut into cubes, to serve

1. Heat the oven to 350°F.

2. Place the dried fruit in a bowl. Add the water, along with 1 teaspoon of baking soda and give the mixture a stir. Let stand overnight to soften.

3. Blend the fruit with the soaking water to make a thick purée. Empty the purée into a large bowl and sift in all the remaining dry ingredients.

4. Blitz the bananas in a food processor until smooth. Slowly add the melted coconut oil until you have an emulsion. Tip into the bowl, along with the other ½ teaspoon of baking soda and the vanilla extract. Fold all the ingredients together, adding almond milk until you have a dropping consistency.

5. Pour the cake batter into a lined 1-pound loaf pan or 8-inch square cake pan and bake in the oven for 30 minutes, then reduce the oven temperature to 325°F and cook for a further 20 minutes.

6. Let cool before removing from the cake pan. Serve with fresh mango.

This would be totally tropical served with grilled pineapple and pineapple, banana, and coconut ice cream (see page 292).

MOIST CHOCOLATE
& ALMOND CUPCAKES

These recipes are from Jane's lovely friend Emily Vevers, who runs Queen Bee Cakes in Devon.
"Moist" is on our funny word list.

PREP TIME: 20 MINS · COOK TIME: 15 MINS

½ cup **coconut oil**, melted, , plus
    extra for greasing

6 oz **sugar-free dark chocolate**

2½ tablespoons **rice flour**

¼ cup **ground almonds**

4 **eggs**

1½ cups **coconut sugar**

½ teaspoon **vanilla extract**

3 tablespoons **water**

dried cherries, finely chopped to
    decorate (optional)

FOR THE FROSTING

3¼ oz **sugar-free dark chocolate**

2 tablespoons **coconut oil**

1 tablespoon **raw honey**

1. Heat the oven to 325°F.

2. Grease 20 holes of two 12-hole mini cupcake pans and line each one with a paper baking cup.

3. Chop the chocolate finely (using a food processor or by hand) and place in a large bowl. Stir in the rice flour and ground almonds and set aside.

4. Beat the eggs and sugar together until pale and fluffy, then set aside.

5. Place the coconut oil, vanilla, and measured water in a pan and bring to a boil. Pour this into the chocolate mixture.

6. Beat together until all the chocolate melts, then let cool. Fold in the egg mixture and divide the batter among the paper baking cups. Bake for 10 to 15 minutes, until well risen and no longer soft to the touch in the middle.

7. Let cool slightly in the pan. When cool enough to handle transfer the cupcakes to a rack to cool completely before adding the frosting.

8. For the frosting, gently melt the chocolate, coconut oil, and honey in a bain-marie. Let cool and solidify slightly, then top each cake with the frosting and decorations of your choice. Leave to set before serving.

These cakes can
be decorated with fresh
summer berries, chopped
pistachio nuts, chocolate curls,
candied orange peel, and lots
more. It's your chance to do
some creative caking.

GRIDDLED PEACHES WITH CASHEW CREAM

Just peachy.

**PREP TIME: 10 MINS · SOAK TIME: OVERNIGHT
COOK TIME: 6 MINS**

1 cup **cashews**, soaked overnight in plenty of **cold water**, then drained

1 teaspoon **vanilla extract**

2 tablespoons **raw honey**

1 cup **raspberries**

juice of 1 **orange**

2 teaspoons **coconut sugar**

4 **peaches**, halved

a drizzle of **amaretto** or **brandy**

¼ cup **almonds**, toasted

1. Blend the nuts in a food processor with about ½ cup water until smooth. Add the vanilla and honey and continue to blend until you have the consistency of very thick cream. Place in the fridge.

2. Blitz the raspberries with the orange juice and sugar. Strain through a sieve or cheesecloth to make a smooth sauce.

3. Heat a griddle until very hot. Place the peach halves, cut-side down, on the griddle and cook for a few minutes, until the peach flesh is charred and caramelized. Transfer to a serving dish.

4. To serve, top the peaches with spoonfuls of cashew cream. Drizzle with raspberry sauce and amaretto, and scatter with toasted almonds to serve.

GOLDEN MERINGUES

Erythritol sounds highly processed, but it's not. (Terrible naming, guys.) Naturally occurring, it has 95 percent fewer calories than sugar.

PREP TIME: 10 MINS · COOK TIME: 1 HOUR 20 MINS

2 **egg whites**

3 tablespoons **erythritol**, ground

few drops of **vanilla extract**

½ teaspoon **cream of tartar**

a pinch of **salt**

You need a dry oven to make meringues. Ideally you shouldn't have cooked anything in it recently.

1. Heat the oven to 250°F.

2. Place all the ingredients in a cold metal or glass bowl. Using an electric mixer, beat together for a few minutes, or until the mixture is stiff and glossy.

3. Spoon small mounds onto a baking pan lined with nonstick parchment paper. Place in the oven and bake for about 20 minutes, then lower the temperature to 225°F and leave in the oven for another hour or so, until the meringues are crisp. The length of time will depend on the exact temperature of your oven.

4. Turn the heat off, but leave the meringues in the oven until they have cooled completely. Serve with peaches and cashew cream, if desired.

CHOCOLATE MAYO BROWNIES

coconut oil, for greasing

9 oz **sugar-free dark chocolate**, chopped into small pieces and melted

3 **eggs**

1 cup **coconut sugar**

½ cup **sugar-free mayonnaise**

⅓ cup **rice flour**

1 teaspoon **baking powder**

½ cup chopped **pecans**

¼ cup **ground almonds**

Before you ask, let us reassure you; these are great. You may not want to tell people what your secret ingredient is, but we think the rich flavor and moist texture that mayo adds beats butter.

PREP TIME: 15 MINS · COOK TIME: 15 MINS

1. Heat the oven to 325°F.

2. Grease an 8½-inch cake pan with coconut oil and line it with nonstick parchment paper (the coconut oil ensures that the parchment paper sticks to the inside of the pan).

3. Cream together the eggs and coconut sugar and beat in the mayonnaise. Fold in the dry ingredients, chopped nuts, and melted chocolate.

4. Pour the cake batter into the pan and bake for about 15 minutes, until just cooked. Remove from the oven and let sit for 5 minutes, then turn out onto a cooling rack. Cut into wedges or squares to serve.

BEANIE (BABY) BROWNIES

9 oz **sugar-free dark chocolate**, broken into small pieces

14 oz can of **cooked navy beans**, drained and rinsed

4 **eggs**

a few drops of **vanilla extract**

1 cup **coconut sugar**

1 teaspoon **baking powder**

These high-protein brownies, pumped up with navy beans, deserve to be honored. A recipe from our friend Meleni Aldridge.

PREP TIME: 15 MINS · COOK TIME: 40 MINS

1. Heat the oven to 325°F.

2. Melt the chocolate in a bowl over simmering water.

3. Blitz the navy beans in a food processor with the eggs and vanilla. Transfer to a bowl, add the sugar and baking powder, and stir well to combine. Stir in the melted chocolate.

4. Pour into a lined 8½-inch square cake pan and bake in the oven for about 20 minutes. Let cool in the pan and, once completely cooled, cut into rectangles to serve.

TREAT YOURSELF

SUMMER SCONES

These rhubarb and strawberry scones will be made today, scone tomorrow. A glorious pun from Polly Richards, a lovely LEON intern.

PREP TIME: 15 MINS · COOK TIME: 15 MINS

1 cup **gluten-free all-purpose flour**

1 cup **ground almonds**

1 tablespoon **modified tapioca starch** (or **baking fix**)

2 teaspoons **baking powder**

¼ cup **coconut oil**

1 cup **coconut sugar**, plus extra for sprinkling

a pinch of **salt**

zest and juice of 1 **orange**

1¼ cups chopped **rhubarb**, cut into ½-inch pieces

½ cup quartered **strawberries**

1 teaspoon **cornstarch**

1 **egg**

2 tablespoons **maple syrup**

3 tablespoons **almond milk**, plus extra for glazing

1. Heat the oven to 400°F.

2. Mix together the flour, ground almonds, starch, and baking powder. Cut the solidified coconut oil into small pieces and rub into the dry ingredients until they resemble bread crumbs. This can also be done in a food processor

3. Grind the coconut sugar until it is fine and stir into the flour and coconut oil mixture along with the salt and orange zest.

4. Toss the rhubarb and strawberries in the cornstarch and stir into the scone mixture.

5. In a measuring cup, beat the egg together with the orange juice and maple syrup until well combined, then add almond milk to the ⅔ cup level. Beat with a fork to combine before adding to the scone mixture. Bring together with a metal spatula to form a very soft dough and then turn it out onto a cookie sheet lined with nonstick parchment paper. Press the dough out into a circle about ½ to ¾ inch thick. Cut into eighths and brush with a little extra almond milk.

6. Sprinkle with the extra coconut sugar and place in the oven for about 15 minutes until golden.

7. Serve warm or at room temperature.

When they are in season, you could also use 2 cups chopped pitted plums instead of the rhubarb and strawberries for this recipe.

LEMON POLENTA CAKE
WITH BLUEBERRIES

The texture of this lemon polenta cake is hard to beat. Crumbly, fluffy, and intense.
You'll be wanting to make polenty.

PREP TIME: 15 MINS · COOK TIME: 30 MINS

1 cup **ground almonds**

1 cup **polenta**

2 tablespoons **cornstarch**, plus
    1 teaspoon

1 teaspoon **baking powder**

½ teaspoon **baking soda**

1 teaspoon **modified tapioca
    starch** (or **baking fix**)

a pinch of **salt**

zest of 2 **lemons**

3 **eggs**

3 tablespoons **brown rice syrup**

3 tablespoons **raw honey**

1 teaspoon **vanilla extract**

3 tablespoons **olive oil**

½ cup **almond milk**

1 cup **blueberries**

1. Heat the oven to 350°F and line an 8½-inch cake pan with nonstick parchment paper.

2. In a large bowl mix together the dry ingredients, except for the 1 teaspoon of cornstarch, and add the lemon zest.

3. Whisk the eggs with the rice syrup and honey until pale. Whisk in the vanilla, olive oil, and milk, then beat the wet mixture into the dry ingredients.

4. Pour the batter into the prepared cake pan. Toss the blueberries in the remaining cornstarch and sprinkle them over the cake mixture. Bake in the oven for 30 minutes.

5. Remove from the oven and let cool in the pan for 10 minutes, then transfer to a cooling rack.

PISTACHIO CAKE
WITH POACHED APRICOTS

Stash a secret slice of this cake somewhere safe or it'll be gone before you've had a chance to tuck in.

PREP TIME: 10 MINS · COOK TIME: 50 MINS

3 **eggs**, beaten

zest of 2 **oranges**

1½ cups **coconut sugar**

⅔ cup **olive oil**

2 cups **ground pistachios**

½ cup **cornmeal**

1 teaspoon **baking powder**

a pinch of **ground cardamom**

1. Heat the oven to 350°F.

2. Line an 8- or 9-inch cake pan with nonstick parchment paper. Beat the eggs with the orange zest and sugar. Add the olive oil and beat to combine.

3. Mix the pistachios with the cornmeal, baking powder, and cardamom and fold them into the egg mixture. Pour the batter into the lined cake pan.

4. Bake for about 50 minutes, or until a skewer inserted in the center comes out clean. Let cool in the pan for 10 minutes, then transfer to a cooling rack.

Cornmeal is like fine polenta—don't get it confused with cornstarch.

POACHED APRICOTS

PREP TIME: 10 MINS · COOK TIME: 5 MINS

3 tablespoons **brown rice syrup**

½ cup **sweet wine**

juice of 1 **orange**

14 oz **fresh apricots**, halved and stone removed

1. Bring the syrup, wine, and orange juice to a simmer. Place the apricots in the syrup and cook for about 5 minutes.

2. Lift the fruit out of the syrup with a slotted spoon and set it aside. Let the syrup continue to simmer until it has reduced by half, about 5 minutes.

3. Pour the syrup over the fruit and serve.

TUSCAN CHESTNUT CAKE

✓

v

Ve

Waste nut want nut. This is a naturally free-from recipe from Tuscany. Be transported to southern Italy. It helps if you have a few sunflowers lying around.

PREP TIME: 10 MINS · COOK TIME: 30 MINS

¼ cup **golden raisins**

vin santo (optional)

2¾ cups **chestnut flour**

a pinch of **salt**

2 tablespoons **brown rice syrup**

2 tablespoons **olive oil**

2 tablespoons **pine nuts**

¼ cup **walnuts**

1 tablespoon coarsely chopped **fresh rosemary leaves**

1. Heat the oven to 350°F.

2. Soak the raisins ahead of time by adding them to a bowl and covering them in hot water, or vin santo or another sweet wine if available.

3. Sift the flour into a large bowl with the salt. Drain the liquid from the raisins into a large measuring cup and make up the amount of liquid to 1¾ cups. Add the liquid to the flour along with the brown rice syrup, beating to combine. Beat in the olive oil and set the batter aside for 30 minutes.

4. Line a 10-inch baking pan with high sides with nonstick parchment paper. Stir half the raisins into the cake batter. The batter should be of pouring consistency, so pour it into the prepared pan to a depth of ¼ inch and sprinkle with the nuts, remaining raisins, and rosemary. Bake in the oven for about 30 minutes. The top of the cake should have a cracked appearance.

5. Remove from the oven and let cool, then cut into slices or squares to serve.

JUMPING JACKS

These nutritious oatmeal squares will have you jumping for joy.

PREP TIME: 15 MINS · COOK TIME: 35 MINS

2 **carrots**

1 **parsnip**

1 **sweet potato**

1 **apple**

½ cup **cashew butter**

¼ cup **rice malt syrup**

½ cup **coconut sugar**

1¼ cups **gluten-free oats**

1 teaspoon **chia seeds**

1 teaspoon **flaxseeds**

1 tablespoon each of **pumpkin** and **sunflower seeds**

½ cup **desiccated coconut**

½ teaspoon **ground cinnamon**

1. Heat the oven to 350°F.

2. Grate all the vegetables and the apple into a large bowl.

3. Melt the cashew butter with the syrup and coconut sugar in a pan over low heat. Add the rest of the ingredients to the grated vegetables. Pour in the melted butter and stir to combine.

4. Line an 8-inch square cake pan or baking pan with nonstick parchment paper. Scrape the mixture into the prepared pan and press it down evenly with the back of a spoon. It should be about ¾ inch deep.

5. Bake for about 30 minutes. Before it has cooled completely, cut into squares to serve.

CHESTNUT CHOCOLATE CHIP COOKIES

Oh, this old chestnut? They're best served warm and gooey.

PREP TIME: 10 MINS · COOK TIME: 15 MINS

2 **eggs**

½ cup **coconut oil**, melted

3 tablespoons **rice malt syrup**

1 teaspoon **vanilla extract**

1 cup **chestnut flour**

½ cup **coconut flour**

1 teaspoon **baking soda**

½ cup **sugar-free dark chocolate chips**

1. Heat the oven to 350°F.

2. Beat the eggs with the oil, syrup, and vanilla in a large bowl.

3. Sift the flours with the baking soda and mix with the wet ingredients. Fold in the chocolate chips.

4. Roll the dough into 12 balls and place on a nonstick cookie sheet, allowing enough space between so the cookies can spread out while baking. Flatten the balls slightly then bake for about 12 to 15 minutes, until golden brown. Let cool before serving.

MINI BOILED CLEMENTINE & ALMOND CAKES

These are based on a recipe by Michelle Cranston, and are great for serving at parties during the holiday season.

PREP TIME: 15 MINS · COOK TIME: 1 HOUR 25 MINS

5 **clementines**

sunflower oil, for greasing

6 **eggs**

1¼ cups **coconut sugar**

a few drops of **vanilla extract**

2 cups **ground almonds**

1 teaspoon **baking powder**

1 **orange**

2 tablespoons **rice malt syrup**

1 teaspoon **poppy seeds**

1. Heat the oven to 350°F.

2. Put the clementines into a pan, cover with water, and let simmer for about 1 hour. Top off the water, if necessary, to ensure the fruit is always covered. Drain and let cool. Add the fruit, including the skin, to a food processor and blend to a purée.

3. Grease 16 muffin pan holes with sunflower oil. Cream the eggs with the sugar and vanilla until pale then stir in the puréed fruit. Fold in the ground almonds and baking powder. Divide the batter among the muffin pan holes and bake in the oven for 20 minutes.

4. Squeeze the orange juice through a sieve and into a small pan over high heat. Add the rice malt syrup and bring the mixture to a boil. Let boil until thick, then set aside. Remove the cakes from the pan while still warm, spoon the orange syrup onto them, and sprinkle with the poppy seeds to serve.

CHRISTMAS PUDDING

Now bring us some figgy pudding, now bring us some figgy pudding, now bring us some figgy pudding, and bring some out here. Jane based this on her sister-in-law Louise's family recipe. It can made made up to three months before Christmas.

PREP TIME: 15 MINS · SOAK TIME: OVERNIGHT · COOK TIME: 7 HOURS

¼ cup **coconut oil**, melted, plus extra for greasing

¾ cup **gluten-free self-rising flour**

¾ cup **ground almonds**

2 tablespoons **psyllium husks**

½ teaspoon **ground nutmeg**

½ teaspoon **ground cinnamon**

½ teaspoon **mixed spice**

¾ lb **mixed dried fruit**

1 cup **coconut sugar**

1 large **carrot**, grated

1 **apple**, grated

¼ cup **gluten-free vegetable shortening**

1 tablespoon **date syrup**

zest and juice of ½ **orange**

zest of 1 **lemon**

1 **egg**

a good slug of **brandy**

1. Mix all the ingredients together and spoon into a greased pudding basin or deep ovenproof bowl. Let stand overnight or for 24 hours, adding more alcohol if you like.

2. Cover the pudding basin or bowl with a layer of nonstick parchment paper and then a layer of foil. Put the bowl into a steamer or saucepan of simmering water, ensuring that the water rises halfway up the side of the pudding basin. Cover and let steam for about 4½ hours, replenishing with boiling water as needed. Let cool, then remove the lid and replace with fresh parchment paper and foil.

3. The pudding can be stored in a cool place. To reheat for serving, steam the pudding, as above, for 2½ hours.

APPLE, DATE & ORANGE CRISP

Resistance is fruitile. This has a very festive flavor, so it's a great hit during the holidays.

PREP TIME: 20 MINS · COOK TIME: 40 MINS

⅓ cup **coconut oil**

1¼ cups **gluten-free all-purpose flour**

¾ cup **gluten-free rolled oats**

1 cup **coconut sugar**, divided

⅔ cup **pecans**, chopped

2¼ lb **apples**, peeled and cored

1 large **orange**

12 **dates**, chopped

2 tablespoons **brandy**

1. Heat the oven to 325°F.

2. Chop the coconut oil into small pieces and rub into the flour until it resembles bread crumbs. This can be done in a food processor.

3. Stir in the oats, half the coconut sugar, and the pecans and rub everything together with your fingertips.

4. Cut the apples into ¾-inch chunks and place in a 10-inch gratin dish or similar shallow baking dish. Zest the orange, remove and discard the peel and pith, and cut the flesh into ¾-inch pieces. Add the zest and fruit to the apples along with the dates, the remaining sugar, and the brandy. Mix together.

5. Top the fruit with the oat and nut mixture and bake in the oven for about 40 minutes. Let cool slightly before serving.

PEAR & CHOCOLATE CAKE

This is another Queen Bee Cakes recipe. The chocolate and the pear make quite a pair.

PREP TIME: 15 MINS · COOK TIME: 45 MINS

1¼ lb **pears** (about 5 large ripe Bartlett pears), peeled and cut into eighths

2 cups **coconut sugar**, plus a little extra for the syrup, divided

¾ cup **coconut oil**, melted

3 medium **eggs**, lightly beaten

zest and juice of 1 **orange**

1 teaspoon **vanilla extract**

1½ cups **self-rising gluten-free flour**, sifted

½ teaspoon **baking powder**

4½ oz **sugar-free dark chocolate**, chopped

FOR THE ICING

1¾ oz **sugar-free dark chocolate**

1 tablespoon **coconut butter**

1 tablespoon **raw honey**

1. Heat the oven to 325°.

2. Grease a 9-inch springform cake pan and line it with nonstick parchment paper.

3. Mix the pears and ¼ cup of the sugar together in a bowl.

4. Beat the remaining sugar, coconut oil, eggs, orange zest, and vanilla together until light and fluffy.

5. Add the flour, baking powder, and chocolate and fold in gently.

6. Place the pear pieces on the bottom layer of the cake pan, arranging them in a spiral pattern. If you have any pear left over, chop into small pieces and add to the cake batter.

7. Spoon the batter into the pan on top of the pears, then place in the middle of the oven and bake for 45 minutes, or until golden and firm to the touch. Bake for an extra 10 to 15 minutes if the cake is still soft in the center. Be careful not to burn the top.

8. While the cake is still warm, unlatch the springform pan and invert the cake onto a large flat plate lined with a sheet of nonstick parchment paper to stop the cake from sticking to the plate. Then carefully peel the parchment paper from the top-side of the cake, using a knife if necessary.

9. Warm the orange juice with a little coconut sugar to make a syrup. Drizzle it over the cake, then let the cake stand to cool on the plate.

10. Melt the icing ingredients in a bain-marie until silky and smooth. Drizzle the icing over the cake, using a pastry brush (in a criss-cross fashion if you're feeling fancy).

11. Let cool before serving.

TREAT YOURSELF

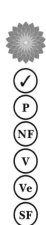

PINEAPPLE, BANANA & COCONUT ICE CREAM

🍽 **4**

A totally tropical treat.

PREP TIME: 5 MINS · FREEZE TIME: 4 HOURS

½ small **pineapple**, peeled
1 large ripe **banana**
1 cup **coconut cream**

1. Dice the flesh of the pineapple into small pieces and slice the banana. Add the mixture to a container and then place in the freezer for at least 4 hours.

2. Drain any watery liquid from the coconut cream and place it in the freezer. It's also a good idea to freeze a glass bowl to serve the ice cream in.

3. Just before serving, blitz everything together until smooth in a food processor or using a hend-held stick blender, pushing down any coarse pieces that creep up the side of the bowl. If you're having trouble blending it, you may have to wait for it to melt slightly before whizzing it in your powerful processor. Serve in the cold glass bowl immediately.

LEON
PALEON BAR

Power up with slow-burning energy that's all hits, no filler. A super hit at our restaurants.

PREP TIME: 10 MINS · COOK TIME: 20 MINS

⅔ cup chopped **dates**

½ cup **water**

a pinch of **vanilla powder**

2 **eggs**

1⅓ cups **ground hazelnuts**

1⅓ cups **ground cashews**

a pinch of **sea salt**

½ cup **coconut oil**, melted but not hot

⅓ cup toasted **pistachios**, coarsely chopped

⅓ cup **cashews**, coarsely chopped

⅓ cup **sunflower seeds**

½ cup **pumpkin seeds**

1½ cups **dried cranberries**

1. Heat the oven to 350°F.

2. Blend the dates, water, and vanilla powder in a high-speed blender until smooth, to make the date paste.

3. Put the date paste into a mixing bowl with the eggs, ground hazelnuts, ground cashews, sea salt, and coconut oil. Stir well to combine, then stir in the chopped nuts, seeds, and cranberries.

4. Press the mixture into an 8-inch square baking pan lined with nonstick parchment paper and bake in the oven for 20 to 22 minutes.

5. Let cool in the pan, then cut into squares.

We love the tartness of dried cranberries but, if you prefer, use currants, raisins, or dried strawberries. To make sure these bars are free from refined sugar, read the ingredients list on the label of your dried fruit to make sure it doesn't contain any added sugar.

RECIPE INDEX

Truffle Parsnip Fries 244
Turkey San Choy Bau 130
Vegetable Harira 110
Vongole 134
Zucchini Salad 232

MAIN INDEX

THANK YOU

FROM JANE

First, thank you to the people of Tokelau (it's where David was made) for being a totally Fast and Free nation and my son David for putting up with a few chaotic months • Rachael—because none of this would have happened without her and at least she didn't throw any essential ingredients down the sink • Emin Cheese—for being cheesy and having the best name • Beth—I have a teeny girl crush because she's so fab (and not the precious fashion idiot I thought she was) • Saskia—for managing us all in a kind of steely determined way and for kicking my ass (again) • Jo—the pizza queen and creative design genius • Tom—for stealing my thunder with the Kofte recipe (and pouncing around being photographed for far too long and loving it) • Tamin—great pics and lovely to work with, although I feel his future is in Page 3 • Steph—a diamond in every respect and a calming influence on us all • Lara and Martin for hosting us at Coombe Farm Studios in Dittisham • Beth and Liam for being fab assistants and choppers extrodinaire • Octopus lot !

FROM JOHN

Until books write themselves (hopefully a long time after cars drive themselves) it takes a lot of people to make a LEON book happen. Jane and I have been so grateful for the love and graft of two people in particular: Saskia and Jo. This love and graft is the basis of an amazing partnership: Saskia is the overall boss and the boss of logistics, editing, and joy, while Jo is the boss of design and art work. Between them they have helped Jane and me make sure the book you have in your hand is our "best" work.

The photography is all down to Tamin Jones whose skill is matched by his character. When you are spending long and yet intense hours with a photographer it makes such a difference when they are positive, can-do, and can bend themselves into lots of different positions (including lying on the ground) in order to show the food in its best light. Thank you Tamin. And thank you too to Tamin's assistant, Steph, who made the photos possible, as well as often making the party.

One of those party places was the comely Coombe Farm in Devon where Lara and her husband Martin hosted us all. I think she enjoyed the upside of eating with us, but went well beyond the norm in showing hospitality (including letting me join the all-female yoga class in my Lycra shorts).

Beth Morgan and Liam Chau were fantastic food assistants.

Thank you too to Millie Hempleman and Tara Hesseltine, who made sure we were all "propped up."

I owe so much too to Wendy Mandy who is a wise, beautiful friend and guide.

Thank you to my many advisers and to people who have backed Leon with their time and counsel: Jane Melvin, Nick Evans, Tim Smalley, Spencer Skinner, Jacques Fragis, Brad Blum, Jimmy Allen, Steve Head, Scott Uehlein, Bob Mock, Mike Ellis, Vivian Imerman and Gavyn Davies.

Meleni Aldridge from Bite the Sun has advised us for the last two years on nutrition, and also wrote the science bits in this book. And Angela Dowden checked all of the nutritional icons, quite a few times.

Carole Symons has, from the beginning of Leon, used all of her scientific and persuasive skills to decry gluten and dairy and sugar.

The shoots needed extra LEON hands and Rachael, Beth, and Emin provided them with vigor.

Our publishing team (or "punk sighing" team as my autocorrect just wrote) is a heavenly group of people led by Alison Starling (who can also be nicely strict) and Jonathan Christie from the creative direction side and Pauline Bache the editor. Thanks too to the PR and marketing teams who have hopefully by now stopped this book from being a secret.

Antony Topping our literary agent has been important to making this happen and has sprayed on the odd WD40 where the process needed it.

All we do now and in the future started in Carnaby Street in 2004 where Henry and Allegra and I began this adventure. Thank you both of you for your support and for all the DNA you (hygienically) injected into LEON. Thank you everyone who works at Leon today and who has been in the gang since 2004.

Thank you Katie for being the most supportive wife a hyperactive man could have and to my fantastic daughters Natasha and Eleanor for your love. My Mom Marion is the most positive person I know and inspires all I do. Well, most of what I do. And of course to my Dad LEON who inspired us a little with our name.

THE LEON FAMILY

Abdelhadi Fekier
Abdullah Mamun
Aboubacar Sanoko
Abril Marcozzi Ahumada
Adam Hon Adam Blaker
Adam Jaworski
Adam Klosowski
Adam Nagy
Ademola Akande
Adetayo John Toye
Adrian Fernandez Jodar
Adrian Pompey
Adriano Paduano
Agnes Hochheiser
Ahmed Ahamada
Ahmed Hussain
Akli Ouarab
Alaina Cisotto
Alan McNiven
Alastair Delaney
Alberto Biasi
Alejandra Martinez
Aleksandra Maj
Alessandro Perleonardi
Alessandro Straccia
Alessia Caberlon
Alessio Marcon
Alex Horwood
Alexander Jean-Baptiste
Alexandra Bacsi
Alexandra Haya
Alexandra Hrinova
Alexandra Liedtke
Alexandrei Lambon
Alexandru Campean
Alexandru Cotici
Alfred Russo
Algirdas Visockis
Alina Leonte
Alisson Grossi
Aljaz Rozenicnik
Allegra Bulferi
Althea Grittini
Alvaro Martin
Amal Noureddine
Amandine Hastoy
Amaury Brusacoram
Amir Astab Hussain
Ana Gututui
Ana Lisman
Ana Minguez
Ana Nobrega Quijano
Ana Pereira Nobrega
Ana Sobrinho

Ana Rita Coelho De Castro
Anabel Guerrero
Anastasija Krickovska
Anderson Gomcalves
Andoni Ibanez Garcia
Andras Klug
Andrea Bassi
Andrea Bulgarelli
Andrea Caratozzolo
Andrea Franchi
Andrea Gil Coll
Andrea Pisci
Andrei Barcau
Andreia Ivascu
Andres Parra Gracia
Angela Antonou
Angelica Vallone
Anna Kormos
Anna Kruk
Anna Llevadias
Anna Swietlicka
Anna Julia Forsell
Palmcrantz
Anna Maria Gioia Ramillano
Antal Babarczi
Anthony Anyetei
Anthony Pierre
Antoinette Xaviera
Antonella Primavera
Antonia Forsythe
Antony Perring
Anwar Sebbah El-Kachachi
Arianna Rosone
Aridane Hernadez
Armani Leroy
Arthur Toso
Arti Dhrona
Asher Spencer
Ashraf Khalifa Mahgoub
Asia Dantoni
Aurelie Diz
Bairish Pushpakanthan
Bartlomiej Chlebanowski
Beatrice Gessa
Ben Iredale
Bence Kovacs
Bernardo Aragao
Bernardo Delgado
Hernandez
Berta Kargaudaite
Bertrand Rameaux
Beth Emmens
Bettina Szabo
Beverley Morgan

Bibiana Adamova
Blanca Lossio Diaz
Blendina Islami
Bola Adako
Borbala Simon
Bouchaib Bouida
Bree Faucher
Brittany Henderson
Bruna Lise De Moura
Caina Bertussi Rotta
Callum Cound
Cameron Essam
Carla Louro
Carlo Poli
Carlos Izquierdo
Carmen Villanueva Garcia
Carolyn Prieur
Cedric Hoffman
Cengiz Rahmioglu
Cesar Alvarez Gallego
Cesar Fernandez
Chad Hyndman
Chanta Octave
Charlene Haughton
Charlene Le Brigand
Charlotte McCarter
Chevonne Robinson
Chiara Donadoni
Chineye Nnamani
Christian Camilli
Christopher Burford
Chuphangini
Chandrakanthan
Cinzia Bastianello
Cinzia Oliviero
Claire Didier
Claire Ollivier
Clara Ballesteros
Clara Bleda Megias
Claudia Costea
Claudia Lagana
Claudinei Da Silva
Cleiton Francisco Da Silva
Clement Claeys
Comfort Babirye
Concetta Arduino
Connor Diver
Cora Forsdick
Corey Douglas
Courtnee Cropp
Craig Wright
Cristina Tonucci
Cristina Tudor
Csaba Borsos

Csaba Lukacs
Daniel Gomez Gomez
Daniela Campos Cruz
Daniela-Claudia Varvarei
Daveline Lionel
David Biro
David Del Rio
David Gera
David O'Leary
Davide Omizzolo
Debbie Thorpe
Debra Maccow
Deepak Lalaji
Denis Rivers Coakley
Desire Bonilla
Desiree Ortiz Saameno
Devni Liyanage
Diane Bolumbo
Dimitar Dimitrov
Djillali Djellal
Dmitrijs Cumacenko
Dmitrijs Iljins
Dominik Bodo
Dora Bleaga
Dovydas Bronusas
Edit Marton
Edson Cadete
Edvinas Marma
El Mehdi Chaouqi
Elin Thomas
Elisa Medd Canete
Elisa Piazza
Elisa Poli
Elisa Pompa
Elizabeth Nobrega Quijano
Elizabeth Olaleye
Elizabeth Oloyede
Elizangela Ravaneda
Elsayed Mohamed
Emanuele Giordano
Emilios Patounas
Emily Hawkley
Emily-Ann Cheese
Emmanuel Saliu
Engila Saidy
Eniolywa Adeyemi
Enrica Latorre
Enrico Bonetti
Erika Fernandez Priegue
Erika Garcia
Erika Gatti
Erika Kupfer
Erika Perna
Erzsebet Hobora

Estibaliz Pena Barbara
Eva Zacharia
Ewan Milne
Ewelina McDonald
Fabio Paixao Da Conceicao Santos
Fabio Prandi
Fabio Rodrigues
Fabio Rosa
Fabio Soliman
Fatma Abdurahman
Federica Masciulli
Federico Bazan
Federico Cau
Felice Catania
Felipe Mesa Koch
Fernando Blanco Gutierrez De Rueda
Filippo Ciarla
Flora Pap
Fontana Clemente
Frances Moran
Francesca Balia
Francesco Basile
Francesco Festevole
Francisco Jimenez San Nicolas
Frederique Anctil
Gabor Salai
Gabriella Kovacs
Gallad Musa
Gary Marriott
Gary Scarboro
Gema Madueno Lada
Gemma Kearney
Georgios Kogkos
Gerard Ribalta I Vivas
Giacomo Medda
Giada Rosignoli
Gianluca Marletta
Gianmarco Abramo
Giorgia Orfei
Giorgia Scaramagli
Giorgio Mancino
Giovanna Fuentes
Giovanna Gargiulo
Giulia Chiominto
Giulia Palmarini
Giuseppe Crielesi
Giuseppe Laporta
Giuseppe Marsiglia
Giuseppi Bargione
Glenn Edwards
Gonzalo Perpina Llorca
Graham Brown
Guido Modena
Gustavo Batistella
Gyongy Matyas
Hafdala Buyema

Hamza Harrat
Hana Abdullah
Hana Pavlovicova
Handan Argun
Hannah Adamson
Hannah Redfearn
Hannah Thomas
Hector Fernandez
Hector Morillo Aguilera
Holly Clare
Hsiang Liao
Ignacio Curtolo
Ilaria De Tommaso
Ina Chiperi
Ines Sineiro
Ines Maria Da Costa De Sepulveda
Ioannis Chaniotakis
Irene Magula
Isabella Noce
Istvan Szep
Iuliana Gaita
Izabela Kaniuk
Jada Kennedy-Mark
Jade Ebejer
Jakub Jacek Adamczewski
James Adewale
Jamie Watts
Jane Eagles
Javier Medina Selles
Javier Santos
Jelena Cumacenko
Jemel Roache
Jenny Di Nunzio
Jesse Jaiquel Martin
Jessica Dolu
Jessica Gonzalez Rios
Jessica Johnstone
Jesus Antonio Tabares Zuniga
Jhun Alkonga
Jimena Del Rosario Cenzano Vicuna
Jiri Czolko
Joanna Buczowska
Joanne Letremy
Jo Ormiston
Joao Freitas
Joao Ribeiro Da Silva
Joao Venda
Joel Brogan
Joelle Bisimwa
Joelle Davis
John Brooks
John Corrigan
John Scott
John Upton
John Vincent
Jorge Palomo Campos

Jorge Valls Laguarda
Jose Maria Arez De Vilhena Alves Rafael
Josep Oriol Ortega Matas
Joshua Prynn-Petit
Judit Alonso Rodriguez
Julio Velezmoro
Justin Ovenden
Justyna Strozyk
Kamila Kilian
Kamran Foladi
Karolina Blazewicz
Kashmira John
Katalin Egyed
Katalin Szabo
Katarzyna Jur
Katia Mendes
Katie Jones
Katya Yovcheva
Kayanda Besa
Kayleigh Goodger
Kelly Coakley
Kelly Lenis Garcia
Kendra Guerrero Marin
Kimberly Ferenc-Batchelor
Kinga Sarvary
Kiril Guglya
Kirsty Adamson
Kirsty Saddler
Kofi Yeboah - Fordjour
Konstantinos Kyziridis
Kristen Rego
Kristina Dabkeviciene
Kristina Kocenaite
Lakshmi Pillay
Larissa Simpson-Brown
Latifah Stone
Laura Espana Saez
Laura Esteban
Laura Stoppini
Layla Mcdougall
Leah Johnson-Nesbitt
Lee Dunning
Lidia Budkowska
Liliya Georgieva
Linda Fischerova
Livio Pierro
Liviu Haulica
Lob Tang
Loredana Tota
Loui-James Lauder
Luca Bargione
Luca Berardi
Luca Galvanelli
Luca La Terra
Luca Lamera
Luca Scazzola
Lucie Schubertova
Lucja Szyszka

Lucrezia Corradi
Lucy Humphrey
Luigi Longobardi
Lukasz Kubiak
Lukasz Ludowich
Lydia Tuker
Lynda Elbounabi
Maciej Kosecki
Maciej Meyza
Maciej Urbanski
Macijauskas Ignas
Magdalena Sierocka
Mahomed Azouz
Maksim Belov
Malgorzata Herda
Malgorzata Pasierb
Manon Joly
Manrique Sancho Caraballeda
Manuel Alvarez Leon
Manuela Crivellari
Marcia Preciosa
Marcin Kaminski
Marco Berardi
Marco Pistilli
Marco Spada
Marcos Diaz-Delgado
Margarita Cadavid Moreno
Maria Belenguer Manzanedo
Maria Cabello Muriana
Maria D'Addio
Maria De Las Heras Bravo
Maria Ghezzi
Maria Reales Garcia
Maria Clara Iudica
Maria Eduarda Moreira
Mariana Kastrati
MariaRosaria Falanga
Marisha David
Marta Konik
Marta Matulewicz
Marta Sedano Vera
Marta Velasco Leonor
Martin Sanchez
Martina Ciccora
Martina Radochova
Martyn Trigg
Mateusz Koziolek
Matteo Di Cugno
Matteo Losito
Matteo Riccobene
Matteo Roscini
Matthew Ali
Matthew Hayden-Baker
Matthew Oakes
Matthew Slaunwhite
Maurizio Ciaburra
Mauro Curtolo

Maxime Roseau
Meenakshi Guirous
Melissa Wilson
Melitta Bicsar
Mercedes Martin
Meymouna Guaye
Michaela Stokoe
Michaela Winter
Michal Urlewicz
Micheline Essomba
Miguel Munoz
Mihaela Sassu
Mihaela Zhivkova
Mirko Antonucci
Mohammed Asmul
Mohammedanwar Sumro
Monica Cardoso
Monika Jagla
Monika Kwiatkowska
Moses Abimbola
Mourad Meghlaoui
Nadea Ahmed
Nadeige Tshiala
Nadiuska De Lourdes
Spranger Santos
Naiara Rodenas Capote
Nainasara Thada Magar
Natalia Kosicka
Natalia Suarez Jimenez
Natalie Birikorang
Natalie Liow
Nataliya Dimitrova
Natasha Cowdrey
Nathan Lewis
Nenko Stoyadinov
Nestor Fernandez
Nhung Le
Nichola Norton
Nicholas Scovell
Nicola Settecase
Nicolas Kupfer Subi
Nikola Vrtiskova
Nikoletta Berta
Nina Amaniampong
Nina Jaworska
Nina Jullien
Niravkumar Desai
Nomsa Mangena
Nora Polacsek
Nundi Parsons
Nunzio Panico
Nuwan Polambe Gedara
Oja Simon
Oktawiusz Kawecki
Olegs Nikolajevs
Olga Chodorowska
Olga Murszakajeva
Oluwatobiloba Olutayo
On Yee Annie Lo

Ona Curto Graupera
Orla Delargy
Orsolya Lazar-Erdelyi
Oskar Zawodniak
Otoa Ise
Ozgur Kuden
Pablo Garcia
Pablo Olalla Vilches
Pascual Micha Avomo
Patricia Rodriguez
Patrick McKenny
Paul Casey
Paul Farmer
Paulo Rodrigues
Pawel Szyszka
Pedro Barchin Perez
Peter Bakai
Peter Meszaros
Petya Zhivkova
Philip Salousti
Philippa Dando
Rabbani Mahbuby
Rabbil Dewan
Rabson Mwale
Rachael Gough
Rachel Austin
Radoslaw Zemsta
Rafael Mendes
Rafal Nowak
Raimundas Melkunas
Raj Halder
Ramona Alexandrescu
Raquel Pascual
Rasa Raskeviciute
Rebeca Calugareanu
Rebecca Di Mambro
Rebecca Kallaghe
Reda el Guebli
Remigijus Chmieliauskas
Remy Le Mentec
Renatas Kacinskas
Rexford Odai
Rhea Peacock
Rianna Alexander-Harris
Ricardo Blanco Sanchez
Ricardo Braun
Ritika Nowlakha
Roberta Adamo
Roberta Bosco
Roberta Rimkute
Roberto Curati
Robinson Garzon
Rodrigo Moreno Fuentes
Romain Brun
Romain Chaillol
Roozbeh Emadmodaresi
Rui Mesquita
Russell Simpson
Rute Valente Coelho Da

Rocha Barreiros
Ruth Chanter
Ruth Johnson-Nesbitt
Ruth Saliu
Sabrina Stefan
Saffron Cann
Salvatore Polizzi
Salvija Dargyte
Sam Kenney-herbert
Samara Addai
Samir Goumrar
Samuel McIntyre
Samuel Rance
Sandra Barriuso
Sandra Navarro
Sara Sanchez Rodrigo
Sarra Tesheme
Saskia Sidey
Sebastian Lapiedra Franco
Sephora Martinez
Serena Bersani
Serena Cecchinato
Serena Micciche
Sergi Cerezo I Martinez
Sergio Garcia Alfaro
Sergio Paniego Blanco
Sergiu Chirilenco
Servet Ozturk
Severina Pascale
Shanti Pun
Sheela Thapa
Shereene Garrison
Shewit Weldegiorgis
Shirine Shah
Shyanne Watson
Sienam Akotey
Silvia Masala
Silvia Zuccarino
Simona Donato
Simona Pugliese
Simona Sodringa
Simone Abbate
Simone Florian
Simone Messina
Simone Pittiglio
Sophie Kaye
Soufian Khatib
Stacey Little
Stacey Strachan
Stefania Paratore
Stefano Pinto
Stephanie Agyemang
Stephen Oliver
Stiven Fernandez
Mondragon
Suada Fetahu
Suna Lee
Szabolcs Szasz
Tadas Tamilinas

Taehoon Jeong
Tamara Hernandez
Tamas Babarczi
Tammy-lee Goodger
Tanya Parratt
Thabiso Moyo
Thiago Turibio Da Silva
Thomas Davies
Thomas Green
Thomas Malley
Thomas Villa
Tierney Faucher
Tom Shephard
Tomas Canet Estornell
Tommaso Marano
Tommaso Venegoni
Tonya Moralez
Tsvetelina Lazarova
Tunde Vig
Ullahelena Wane Ndembo
Vaiva Gaudutyte
Valentin Dragan
Valentino Esposito
Valeria Angelova
Valeria Colesanti
Vanessa Dos Santos
Vanessza Kobli
Vasilica Cirican
Vendella Bubu-
Oppenheimer
Vendula Kozova
Veronica Scotto Di Perta
Victoria Kuziora
Vieri Martini
Viktor Kanasz
Viktorija Kapustina
Vito Rubino
Viviane Bogdanov Simao
Vivien Walker
Vuyolwethu Vundla
Wanda Perretta
William Caddick
Wojciech Antoniewicz
Yasmin Mesquita
Yasmine Rajim
Yemima Walet Ibrahim
Yenny Chong
Ylenia Bermudez Sanchez
Zahidul Islam
Zara Mughal
Zaynab Ali
Zilvinas Gryte
Zoe Cuartas
Zoe Grant
Zoe Masson-Herve
Zsofia Szabo
Zsuzsanna Szalkai
Zunezo Sadiq
Zydrune Petrauskaite

An Hachette UK Company
www.hachette.co.uk

First published in Great Britain in 2017 by Conran Octopus,
a division of Octopus Publishing Group Ltd
Carmelite House, 50 Victoria Embankment
London EC4Y 0DZ
www.octopusbooks.co.uk
www.octopusbooksusa.com

Text copyright © LEON Restaurants Ltd 2017
Design and layout copyright © Octopus Publishing Group 2017

Distributed in the US by Hachette Book Group
1290 Avenue of the Americas
4th and 5th Floors, New York, NY 10104

Distributed in Canada by Canadian Manda Group
664 Annette Street, Toronto, Ontario, Canada M6S 2C8

ISBN 978-1-84091-732-1

A CIP catalogue record for this book is available
from the British Library.

Printed and bound in China

10 9 8 7 6 5 4 3 2

PHOTOGRAPHY BY TAMIN JONES

Publisher: Alison Starling
Senior editor: Pauline Bache
Art direction, styling and design (for LEON): Jo Ormiston
Creative director: Jonathan Christie
Copywriter and brand manager (for LEON): Saskia Sidey
Recipe nutritional analysis: Angela Dowden
Additional "Why Free-from" text: Meleni Aldridge
Photography assistant: Stephanie Howard
Copyeditor: Annie Lee
Senior production manager: Katherine Hockley

We have endeavored to be as accurate as possible in all the
preparation and cooking times listed in the recipes in this
book. However they are an estimate based on our own timings
during recipe testing, and should be taken as a guide only,
not as the literal truth. The nutritional advice given here
is not absolute. If you feel you require consultation with a
nutritionist, consult your family physician or healthcare
provider first.

Eggs should be medium-size unless otherwise stated. The
Food and Drug Administration advises that certain people,
including children, older adults, pregnant women, and people
with weakened immune systems should avoid consuming
raw or lightly cooked eggs, and should use pasteurized eggs/
egg products when preparing recipes that call for raw or
undercooked eggs. Once prepared these dishes should be kept
refrigerated and used promptly.

Fresh herbs should be used unless otherwise stated. If
unavailable use dried herbs as an alternative but halve the
quantities stated.

Ovens should be preheated to the specific temperature. If
using a convection oven, follow manufacturer's instructions for
adjusting the time and the temperature.

This book includes dishes made with nuts and nut derivatives.
It is advisable for customers with known allergic reactions to
nuts and nut derivatives and those who may be potentially
vulnerable to these allergies, such as pregnant and nursing
mothers, invalids, the elderly, babies and children, to avoid
dishes made with nuts and nut oils. US law requires that labels
must clearly identify the food source names of all ingredients
that are (or contain any protein derived from) the eight most
common, major food allergens. Be sure to read the labels
of ready-made ingredients for the possible inclusion of nut
derivatives.

Vegetarians should look for the American Vegetarian
Association (AVA) "Certified Vegetarian" symbol before
buying cheese to ensure it is made with vegetarian rennet.

Not all soy sauce is gluten-free. We use tamari (a gluten-free
type of soy sauce), but check the label if you are unsure.

Remember to check the labels on ingredients to make sure
they don't have hidden refined sugars. Even savory foods can
be artificially sweetened, so it's always best to check the label
carefully.

ABOUT THE AUTHORS
JANE BAXTER

Jane Baxter is the co-author of *Leon Happy Salads* with John
Vincent and *Leon Fast Vegetarian* with Henry Dimbleby. She
also co-authored *The Riverford Farm Cook Book*, which won Best
First Book at the Guild of Food Writers' Awards. Jane worked
at the Carved Angel in Dartmouth and the River Cafe London
before becoming the Head Chef at the Field Kitchen, the
restaurant for Riverford Organic Vegetables. She now spends
her time catering, consulting on food matters and hosting
food events in unusual locations.

JOHN VINCENT

John Vincent is the Co-founder of Leon, which now has more
than 45 restaurants across the UK. He wrote the bestselling
Leon Naturally Fast Food with Henry Dimbleby, *Leon Family &
Friends* with Kay Plunkett-Hogge and *Leon Happy Salads* with
Jane Baxter. John co-wrote the Government's School Food
Plan, with Leon co-founder Henry Dimbleby, which resulted in
practical cooking and nutrition being put on the curriculum
for the first time, and free school lunches for all infant
children. John likes food, and Jane.